M000280237

Contains more than 2,000 Holy Ghost originated Life-changing Prayer Points touching on all aspects of life, and relevant to our time and environment.

PRAY YOUR WAY

TO

BREAKTHROUGHS

DR. D. K. OLUKOYA

Revised and Enlarged Edition

II

© MFM 1996
PRAY YOUR WAY TO BREAKTHROUGHS
Dr. D. K. OLUKOYA

A publication of:
Mountain of Fire and Miracles Ministries

Lagos, Nigeria Address
13, Olasimbo Street, off Olumo Road,
(By UNILAG Second Gate)
Onike, Iwaya
P. O. Box 2990, Sabo, Yaba, Lagos.

London Address
Battersea Chapel,
WYE Street,
Battersea,
London SWII 2SR
Telephone:0171-2286407

Cover designed by: Sister F. Olukoya

ISBN 978-978-2947-00-0

PRAY YOUR WAY TO BREAKTHROUGHS
Dr. D. K. OLUKOYA

Eleventh Edition – August, 2009
Twelfth Edition – October, 2010

Printed by PRINTCORP. LP # 02330/0494142 of 03.04.2009.
40 Skorina St., Minsk 220141. Belarus. Order. 2803 (10157). Qty 10 000.

DEDICATION

This Prayer Book is dedicated to Late Apostle Joseph Ayo Babalola, a minister of God who understood the power of prayer. He was the man mightily used by God to ignite the fire of the first Christian revival in this country in the nineteen thirties.

Brother J. A. and his team of aggressive prayer warriors entered forbidden forests, silenced demons that demanded worship, paralysed deeply-rooted anti-gospel activities. Sometimes beginning from the highest places, emptied hospitals by the healing power of the Lord Jesus Christ, rendered witchdoctors jobless and started the first indigenous Holy-Ghost filled church in Nigeria. So far - and we stand to be corrected - none has equalled, let alone surpassed this humble Brother in the field of aggressive evangelism in this country.

O thou that hearest prayer, unto thee shall all flesh come.

How To Use This Book

Prayer is a gift to you and a privilege. The gift of prayer is offered to all and all may become the wielders of the great powers in prayer. However, the fact remains that the power of prayer is the power which is least exercised by the average believer. You will do well to learn the science of warfare prayer. The present temperature of the prayers of many christians will need to rise if they expect serious breakthroughs.

This set of prayers is targeted towards certain needs so that your praying will not be as one beating the air. This is how to go about using the booklet:

(1)   Locate your area of need by looking at the table of contents.

(2)   Select appropriate scriptures promising you what you desire. Meditate on these and let them sink into your spirit.

(3)   Go about the prayers in any of the following ways as led by the Holy Spirit:

      (a)   3 days' night vigil i.e praying from 10 P.M. to 5 A.M for three consecutive days.

      (b)   3 days' fast (breaking daily) i.e praying at intervals and breaking the fast at 6.00 PM or 9.00. PM daily.

      (c)   7 days' night vigil i.e praying from 10 PM. to 5 AM for seven consecutive days.

      (d)   7 days' fast (breaking daily) i.e praying at intervals and breaking the fast at 6.00 PM or 9.00.PM daily.

O thou that hearest prayer, unto thee shall all flesh come.

(e)   3 or more days of dry fast.i.e praying and fasting for three days without any food or drink.

(4)   Pray aggressively.

NOTE: "Pray In The Spirit" - Praying in the Spirit is an ability to pray in tongues as given utterance by the Holy Spirit. To pray in the Spirit, you must have been baptised in the Holy Ghost (not water baptism) - 1Cor. 14:15.

You will be victorious in Jesus' name.

O thou that hearest prayer, unto thee shall all flesh come.

CONTENTS

O thou that hearest prayer, unto thee shall all flesh come.

VIII

O thou that hearest prayer, unto thee shall all flesh come.

O thou that hearest prayer, unto thee shall all flesh come.

X

O thou that hearest prayer, unto thee shall all flesh come.

O thou that hearest prayer, unto thee shall all flesh come.

XII

O thou that hearest prayer, unto thee shall all flesh come.

PRAYERS OF THANKSGIVING AND PRAISES

Psalm 50:23: Whoso offereth praise glorifieth me: and to him that ordereth his conversation aright will I shew the salvation of God.

At the beginning of your prayer, set aside some time to specifically praise God.

SONGS OF THANKSGIVING AND PRAISES

(i)   Holy, Holy, Holy (Hymn)

(ii) This is the day

(iii) Worthy is the Lamb

(iv) The Lion of Judah

(v)   How Great Thou Art (Hymn)

(vi) Jesus, we enthrone You

(vii) The steadfast love of the Lord

(viii) Count your blessings (Hymn)

PRAYER POINTS

1. Lord, I magnify and praise Your name for calling me to be an heir of Your eternal kingdom.

2. Lord, I bless You for Your hand upon my life and for keeping me underneath Your everlasting arms.

Prayer is the Master Key to open all closed doors.

3. Father, I give You devout and humble thanks for the great gift of Jesus Christ.
4. I thank You Lord for the presence of the Holy Spirit within me.
5. I praise You Lord for:
   (i)   the life that is within me
   (ii) keeping me undevoured in the midst of the world's wicked fire
   (iii) putting the enemy's gear on reverse
   (iv) past blessings You have bestowed upon me.
6. Almighty Father, I thank You for all things work together for good on my behalf.
7. O Lord, I thank You for the blessedness of Your presence.
8. I bless and adore Your holy name for You have called me to be a member of the Church of Christ.
9. I thank You Lord, for the consciousness of divine fellowship and for strengthening me against temptation.
10. I praise You Lord for:
    (i)   hell is vanguished and death is dead
    (ii)   turning my sorrow into gladness
    (iii) turning pain into victory
    (iv)   robbing sin of its power
    (v)   the new life offered to me
    (vi)   the power that keeps me when asleep
    (vii) for Your name which is highly lifted up - wonderful, counsellor, the mighty God, etc (Psalm 115:1)
    (viii) for Your righteousness (Psalm 35:28)
    (ix)   for Your mighty acts and creative power (Psalm 150:2)
    (x)   for Your infinite Word (Psalm 56:10).
11. I thank You for Your prophets and preachers through whom I have learnt something of Your heart.

Prayer is the staff to walk with God and to fight with the devil.

12. Lord, teach me to worship and adore You.
13. Lord, teach me to magnify You.

This is basically a guideline.

Remember,

1. Our God has no limit, our praise is limitless.
2. Give thanks always for all things (Eph. 5:20).
3. Praise is the highest occupation of angels.
4. Praise decentralizes self.
5. Satan is allergic to praise.
6. Praise must be aggressive, purposeful and perpetual.
7. Praise is a spiritual detergent purifying faith and purging doubt.
8. Praise involves responding to God for what He has done.
9. Praise is exalting God and proclaiming His greatness.
10. Praise focuses upon God.
11. Praise speeds victory in your prayer battles.
12. Praise strikes terror into the camp of the enemy.
13. Praise multiplies faith and washes the spirit.
14. Praise is our response to God for Who He is, while thanksgiving is our response to what He has done.

PRAYERS OF FORGIVENESS

Psalm 51: Vs.1-3: Have mercy upon me, O God, according to thy lovingkindness: according unto the multitude of thy tender mercies blot out my transgressions. Wash me thoroughly from mine iniquity, and cleanse me from my sin. For I acknowledge my transgressions: and my sin is ever before me.

PRAYER POINTS

1. Lord, I acknowledge my faults and failures before You.
2. Lord, let me keep nothing hidden from You as I pray.
3. Lord, let me not express shame to confess what I did not express shame to committ.
4. Lord, I am sorry for all the times I have betrayed the trust You have given me to keep.
5. Lord, I acknowledge before You and I ask You to forgive my
    1) self-deception
    2) failure to live according to Your standard
    3) hardness of heart in any form
    4) doubt
    5) failure to attain the standard of conduct I demand of others
    6) speaking in hastiness
    7) failure of self-control
    8) procrastination and loitering

A Christian is greatest on his knees.

9) being a stumbling block to someone else
10) loosing important opportunity
11) alowing my mind to wander to dirty ways
12) concealing my real motives
13) pretending to be better than I am
14) deceitful heart and crooked thoughts
15) speaking thoughtless words
16) lukewarmness to witnessing
17) inadequate praying
18) inadequate reading of the Bible
19) inadequate watchfulness
20) blindness of the heart towards perishing souls
21) laziness
22) vanity
23) indulgence of the flesh
24) habit of falsehood
25) dishonesty
26) uncharitable pronouncement
27) evil thoughts
28) spiritual lapses
29) lukewarmness
30) living above one's spiritual experience
31) unsatisfactory usage of the talent You gave to me
32) unprofitable avoidance of necessary duty
33) my jealousy of those whose lots are easier.

6. Let Your Spirit rule more and more in my heart giving me victory over all sinful ways.
7. O Lord, save me and blot out my iniquities.
8. Create in me a clean heart, o God.

Prayer is the strength of weakness.

9. Father drown my trangression in the sea of Your love in the name of Jesus.
10. Lord, deliver me from any false reliance upon my own strength.
11. Father, I pray that shame will never keep me from confessing my sins in the name of Jesus.
12. O Lord, order my steps and let not any iniquity have dominion over me.
13. O Lord, set a watch on my mouth and help me to keep the door of my lips.
14. I confess to the sin of . . . in the name of Jesus. (*List specific sins that you know.*)
15. Lord, blot out all my trangressions and wash my sins away.
16. Lord, let Your hand of fire cleanse me from the stain of past misdeeds.
17. Lord, let Your fire loose me from the grip of evil habits.
18. Father, help me to let Christ be for real in my heart through faith in the name of Jesus.
19. Lord, guide my footsteps in the way of eternal life.
20. Lord, help me to strengthen my hold upon eternal life.
21. All selfish and worldly-minded schemes will not prosper in my life in the name of Jesus.

3 KILL THEIR PROPHETS

Recommended for those who (i) received the ministry of satanic prophets or (ii) collected negative clinical prophecies or (iii) received curses by fake prophets.
Scripture Reading: 2 Kings 10:12-28
Confession: Isa. 8:9,10

PRAYER POINTS
1. Pray with gratitude for the Cross.
2. Thank God for Christ's redemptive suffering.
3. Lord, remove whatever is keeping me from being the best for You.
4. I command the spirit of confusion to come upon all satanic prophets hired against me in the name of Jesus.
5. I silence every prophet of doom targetted against my life in the name of Jesus.
6. The Lord should bring to naught all evil counsellors and counsels against me.
7. The Lord should coat my name with fire and favour.
8. I command anything growing or present in my life contrary to the will of God to die in the name of Jesus.
9. I silence every false prophet in this nation in the name of Jesus.
10. The Lord should slay every false prophet hired against my life in Jesus' name.

Satan trembles when he sees the weakest saint upon his knees.

Recommended for those surrounded by enemies warring against their breakthroughs.
Scripture Reading: Hebrews 4
Confession: Psalm 18:29

PRAYER POINTS

1. Thank God for the convicting work of the Holy Spirit that led you to turn from your sins to Jesus.
2. The Lord should open my eyes to see the table that He has set before me.
3. Let the mischief of the enemy return upon his own head, in Jesus' name.
4. The Lord should ordain His arrows against my persecutors.
5. The Lord should empower me to run through the troops standing against my blessing in Jesus' name.
6. The Lord should render to no effect every device of the devil against me.
7. Lord, pour down the anointing to prosper upon me.
8. Lord, renew my strength and fortify my spirit.
9. No power from the bottom of the pit will slow down my progress in the name of Jesus.

Recommended for those who are struggling to cross specific, formidable hurdles in order to receive their miracles.
Scripture Reading: Psalm 18
Confession: Numbers 23:23

PRAYER POINTS

1. Thank God for His many gifts to you and your household.
2. The Lord should give me power to mount on wings like eagles.
3. Pray for a deep, holy hunger for God's truth.
4. Pray for someone you know that needs to know the peace of Christ.
5. That the Lord should enable me to hear His direction correctly.
6. Let all the enemies of my soul be confounded in the name of Jesus.
7. The Lord should empower me to leap over all the walls of difficulties constructed by the enemy.
8. The Lord should convert my adversity to triumph in the name of Jesus.
9. The Lord should convert my defeat into victory.
10. The Lord should give unto me the Spirit of Revelation and Wisdom.

Prayer can do all that God is able to do.

BREAK
A
BOW OF
STEEL

Recommended for those whose strength needs to be fortified before they face a particular difficult problem.
Scripture Reading: 1 Sam. 5:1-10
Confession: Psalm 18:34

PRAYER POINTS

1. Thank God for the goodness and benefits we receive day by day.
2. Every weapon of wickedness fashioned against me will not function in the name of Jesus.
3. The Angels of the living God should chase every evil arrow fixed at me back to the senders.
4. Pray with gratitude for the victory won for us at Calvary.
5. Pray that God should call out many workers for His Church.
6. Pray that the Lord should be the Director of your thoughts as well as your paths.
7. That God will make your tongue dance to the tune of wisdom and kindness.
8. Pray for financial breakthrough.
9. Pray that all the days of your life will be dedicated to God.
10. Lord, make me a channel of Your peace and deliverance.

Prayer succeds when all other things fail.

Recommended for those whose names are being circulated for evil purposes and those threatened by envious satanic agents.
Scripture Reading: Acts 8, Hosea 10:2, Judges 6:25-32
Confession: Obadiah 1:3,4

PRAYER POINTS

1. Praise the Lord because the gates of hell shall not prevail against His church.
2. Let the fire of God fall down and consume every altar of false religion in this countryin the name of Jesus.
3. Let every blood-drinking demon be bound and rendered completely incapacitated in the name of Jesus.
4. Let every altar of witchcraft and familiar spirit, be broken in the name of Jesus.
5. We set the fire of God on demon powers eating sacrifices on cross roads.
6. I command that every altar of wickedness constructed against me to be broken in the name of Jesus.
7. Lord, release Your wonder-working Power upon Your Church.
8. Let every tongue contrary to my peace be permanently silenced in the name of Jesus.
9. Pray in the Spirit for at least 30 minutes (See note on how to use this book - page vi)

The spirit of prayer is the spirit of revival.

SLAY THE GIANTS

Scripture Reading: 1 Sam. 17, Joshua 14
Confession: Jer. 1:19

PRAYER POINTS

1. Thank God for His love to you.
2. Let every satanic giant standing against me begin to fall after the order of Goliath in the name of Jesus.
3. Reveal the secret of every hidden giant to me in the name of Jesus.
4. Let me experience Your Power and Victory in every area of my life.
5. Let the Holy Spirit take perfect control of my tongue.
6. Give me the grace to express Your love to the needy.
7. I command all contrary trees growing in my business to be uprooted and be cast into the fire in the name of Jesus.
8. I command every mountain of problem (in whatever area of my life) to move and be cast into the sea in the name of Jesus.
9. Lord, make me Your battle axe.
10. Lord, bless my work with Your prosperity.

Prayer is God's method.

LOOSE THEM AND BRING THEM TO ME

Prayers to release imprisoned blessings.
Scripture Reading: Matthew 21:1-11
Confession: Psalm 71:21

PRAYER POINTS

1. Give thanks as the Holy Spirit leads you.
2. Lord, rain abundant blessings over me in the name of Jesus.
3. Make this year a year of the beginning of great things in my life in the name of Jesus.
4. From the North, South, East and West, let all my blessings be released and let them come unto me.
5. Let my stolen blessings be restored to me seven-fold in Jesus' name.
6. Lord, increase the anointing of the Holy Spirit upon my life.
7. I loose myself from any bondage in the name of Jesus.
8. Let this programme be converted to testimonies in my life in the name of Jesus.
9. Lord, condition my life to live in Canaan now.
10. Praises.

God does nothing but by prayer and everything with it.

PURSUE, OVERTAKE AND RECOVER

Scripture Reading: 1 Sam. 30
Confession: Psalm 18:37

PRAYER POINTS

1. Thank God for His love, and mercy on you.
2. Praise the Lord with this chorus: "Who is like unto Thee . . .?"
3. The Lord should ordain terrifying noises unto the camp of the enemies of the gospel in my life (II Kings 7:6,7).
4. I command every satanic embargo on my goodness and prosperity to be scattered to irreparable pieces in the name of Jesus.
5. Let every door of attack on my spiritual progress be closed in Jesus' name.
6. Holy Spirit, set me on Fire for God.
7. I command all my imprisoned benefits to be released in Jesus' name.
8. The Lord should anoint me to pull down negative strongholds standing against me.
9. Let the thunder fire of God strike down all demonic strongholds manufactured against me.
10. The Lord should anoint me with the power to pursue, overtake

---

Prayer is the hand that strikes down satan.

and recover my stolen properties from the enemy.

11. The Lord should bring to naught every evil counsellor and counsel against me.

12. The enemy shall not have a hiding place in my life in Jesus' name.

13. Let all blocked ways of prosperity be open up in Jesus' name.

14. I command the devil to take his legs off my finances in Jesus' name.

15. I paralyse every spirit of Goliath with the stones of fire in the name of Jesus.

16. Pray in the Spirit for at least fifteen (15) minutes.

17. I command every demonic transport vehicle loading away my benefits to be paralysed in the name of Jesus.

18. I receive the power to pursue every stubborn pursue into the red sea in the name of Jesus.

19. Let the mandate issued to every robber of my blessing be rendered null and void in the name of Jesus.

20. O Lord, provide me with the Moses to face my Pharaoh and the David to face my Goliath.

21. Let the wheels of all pursuing evil chariots be chattered in the name of Jesus.

22. I pursue and overtake all forces of household wickedness and I recover my stolen items from them in the name of Jesus.

23. Let blessings, goodness and prosperity pursue and overtake me in the mighty name of Jesus.

24. I command all my properties captured by spiritual robbers in the dream to become too hot to handle and to come back to me in the name of Jesus.

Every great movement of God can be traced to a knelling figure.

Prayer to find out secret things from the Lord.
Scripture Reading: Daniel 2
Confession: Daniel 2:2, Eph. 1:17

PRAYER POINTS

1. Thank God for the Holy Spirit.
2. Lord give unto me the Spirit of revelation and wisdom in the knowledge of Yourself.
3. The Lord should remove spiritual cataract from my eyes.
4. Lord, forgive me for every false motive or thought that has ever been formed in my heart since the day I was born.
5. Lord, forgive me for any lie that I have ever told against any person, system or organisation.
6. Lord, deliver me from the bondage and sin of spiritual laziness.
7. Lord, open up my understanding.
8. Lord, teach me deep and secret things.
9. Lord, reveal to me every secret behind any problem that I have.
10. Lord, should bring to the light every thing planned against me in darkness.
11. The Lord should ignite and revive my beneficial potentials.
12. Ask the Lord for divine wisdom to operate your life.

Prayer is releasing the energies of God.

13. The Lord should make His Church a citadel of holiness, wonder, miracle and glory upon the earth.

14. God should bring the workers of His choice to His Church and keep all other evil agents away.

15. O Lord, let every veil preventing me from having plain spiritual vision be removed .

16. Father in the name of Jesus, I ask to know Your mind about . . . (*slot in the appropraite situation*) situation.

17. Let the spirit of prophesy and revelation fall upon the totality of my being in the name of Jesus.

18. Holy Spirit, reveal deep and the secret things to me about . . .

19. I bind every demon that pollutes spiritual vision and dreams in the name of Jesus.

20. Let every dityness blocking my communication pipe with the living God be washed clean with the blood of Jesus.

21. I receive power to operate with sharp spiritual eyes that cannot be deceived in the name of Jesus.

22. Let the glory and the power of the Almighty God fall upon my life in a mighty way in the name of Jesus.

23. I remove my name from the book of those who grope and stumble in darkness in the name of Jesus.

24. O Lord, make me a vessel capable of knowing Your secret things.

25. Divine revelations, spiritual visions, dreams and informations will not become scarce commodity in my life in the name of Jesus.

26. I drink to the full in the well of salvation and anointing in the name of Jesus.

27. Pray in the spirit for at least 15 minutes before going to bed.

Prayer is releasing the energies of God.

AVENGE ME OF MINE ADVERSARIES

Scripture Reading: Luke 18:1-7
Confession: Psalm 18:45-47

PRAYER POINTS

1. Praise the Lord because the gates of hell shall not prevail against His Church.
2. Thank the Lord for His promises that are Yea and Amen.
3. Thank the Lord for purchasing victory for us with His Blood.
4. The Lord should turn me into hot coals of untouchable fire.
5. I command every form of demonic family bondage to break in Jesus' name.
6. I loose myself from the hold and influence of every ancestral spirit in Jesus' name.
7. I command every bad spiritual deposit in my life to be melted away by the fire of the Holy Ghost.
8. I bind all the suckers of peace and happiness in my house in Jesus' name.
9. I retrieve my blood or any other material from my body from every evil altar.
10. I loose myself from every linkage to any family idol in Jesus' name.

Prayer is the gateway of God's presence.

11. I bind every spirit of infirmity in the name of Jesus.
12. Let every tongue contrary to my peace be permanently silenced in the name of Jesus.
13. Let every altar of witchcraft, familiar spirits and false religion be broken in this country in the name of Jesus.
14. Every weapon of wickedness being fashioned against me will not function in Jesus' name.
15. Let every evil imagination against me fail woefully in Jesus' name.

Scripture Reading: Proverbs 4
Confession: Jer. 17:14

PRAYER POINTS

1. Give thanks as the Holy Spirit leads you.
2. Lord, cleanse me from every filthiness of the spirit.
3. The Lord should promote me from minimum to maximum in all spheres of my life in Jesus' name.
4. I shall not labour in vain nor bring forth for trouble in the name of Jesus.
5. Every good thing that my hands have laid its foundation shall be completed finished by my hands in Jesus' name.
6. I shall find favour in my going out and my coming in the name of Jesus.
7. Let every evil device against my health be disappointed in the name of Jesus.
8. I reject and denounce every spirit of failure.
9. Lord, let holiness unto You be my watchword and my lot.
10. I overthrow the citadel of sickness, weakness and fear in my life in Jesus' name.
11. Let me be transfused with the Blood of the Lord Jesus Christ.

The tongue of fire is obtained in the prayer room.

12. Lord, clothe me with the mantle of fire.
13. I reject every spiritual invitation to oppressors in my body in Jesus' name.
14. Lord, make me Your battle axe.
15. Lord, give me the grace to live in divine health.

DEATH TO THE PHARAOHS AND HERODS

Spiritual Pharaohs are forces of the stubborn pursuers while spiritual Herods are the forces that destroy good things in infancy and also the prophet killers.

Scripture Reading: Exodus 14, Acts 12:21-24

Confession: Isa. 54:14,15 Jer. 46:17

PRAYER POINTS

1. Thank God who daily loads us with benefits.
2. Let every satanic giant standing against me begin to fall after the order of Goliath in the name of Jesus.
3. Let all diviners and enchanters hired against me fall after the order of Balaam in the name of Jesus.
4. Let all giants standing against peace and unity in my home fall and die in Jesus' name.
5. I bind and set ablaze every spirit of marriage destruction.
6. Let all my Pharaohs perish in the Red sea in the name of Jesus.
7. Let all my Herods be devoured by spiritual worms in the name of Jesus.
8. Woe unto the spirit that turns into cows, elephants, masquerades or any other object in order to hinder my blessings.
9. Lord, release Your wonder-working power upon Your Church.

Where there is no prayer, there is no power.

10. Lord, multiply Your flock in every Church of God by Your Mighty Hand.
11. Lord, set my spirit on Fire for You.
12. Lord, fill me to the brim with Your power.
13. Let every architect of spiritual coffins enter therein themselves in the name of Jesus.
14. I command the stronghold of fear, worry and anxiety to be pulled down in my life in Jesus' name.
15. Let all drinkers of blood and the eaters of flesh eat their own flesh and drink their own blood in the name of Jesus.

Prayer is omnipotent.

DECREE BREAKTHROUGHS

Scripture Reading: Lamentation 3
Confession: Psalm 16:6

PRAYER POINTS

1. Thank God for His unfailing love.
2. The Lord should open up the pipeline of prosperity into my handiwork and my business.
3. I bind every spirit of financial failure in the name of Jesus.
4. Lord, loose the Spirit of prosperity upon me.
5. Lord, anoint me with the power to prosper.
6. I declare this year a year of super abundance for me in the name of Jesus.
7. Lord, give me a breakthrough of blessing in the spiritual, financial, marital and business life.
8. Let the Holy Spirit take perfect control of my tongue.
9. Lord, give me the grace to express Your love to the needy.
10. I command every contrary tree growing in my life to be uprooted and thrown into the fire.
11. Lord, rain abundant blessings upon me in Jesus' name.
12. Lord, make this programme the beginning of great blessings in my life in Jesus' name.

Prayer moves the hand that moves the world.

13. From the North, South, East and the West, let all my blessings be released and let them come unto me.

14. I decree that my stolen blessings should be restored seven-folds.

15. Let every evil attachment to my place of birth be disrupted in the name of Jesus.

16. I command every agent acting against my breakthroughs to be permanently paralysed in the name of Jesus.

17. I command every power barking against my progress to be silenced in the name of Jesus.

18. I receive the anointing for supernatural breakthroughs in all my endavours in the name of Jesus.

19. I receive the anointing of the beautiful feet and the prospering hand in the name of Jesus.

Prayer is the refuge of affliction.

Scripture Reading: Mark 9:1-10
Confession: Psalm 61:2,3

PRAYER POINTS

1. Praise the Lord because the gates of hell shall not prevail against His Church.
2. Thank God for the benefits you have received and will receive from this programme.
3. Let the precious Blood of Jesus cleanse my body, soul and spirit of all contrary marks.
4. Lord, convert my desert to fruitful land.
5. Lord, convert my adversity to triumph.
6. Lord, convert my minimum to maximum.
7. Lord, convert my scars to stars.
8. Lord, convert my defeat into victory.
9. Pray that all the days of your life will be dedicated to God.
10. Lord, lead me to the rock that is higher than I.
11. I fire back all arrows, enchantments and spells issued against me or any member of my family in the name of Jesus.
12. Lord, place me on the mountain of fire and miracles.
13. Lord, I ask for power and wisdom to run the race set before me.
14. Lord, let this programme be converted to testimonies in my life.

Prayer is fellowship with God.

Prayers to remove stubborn mountains and cast them into the sea of forgetfullness.
Scripture Reading: Isa. 37
Confession: Isa. 12:2,3

PRAYER POINTS

1. Thank God for Calvary and for His redemptive work on you.
2. Battle against the spirit of the valley.
   Instructions:
   (a) *Call the spirits you do not desire in your life.*
   (b) *Then issue the command firmly and repeatedly that the spirit must come out in the name of the Lord Jesus Christ.*
   (c) *Then take 3 or 4 slow deep breaths, determinedly expelling them.*
3. *Pray as follows:* You spirit of . . ., I loose myself from you in the name of Jesus, and command you to leave me right now in the name of Jesus.
4. *Now, attack the underlisted spirits one by one following the above instructions.*

Prayer is the wealth of poverty.

1. Spiritual laziness	11. Confusion	21. Infirmity
2. Self-pity	12. Destruction	22. Selfishness
3. Worry	13. Death	23. Rejection
4. Failure	14. Discouragement	24. Wounded Spirit
5. Fear	15. Unbelief	25. Malice
6. Envy	16. Addiction	26. Mind blanking
7. Tension	17. Weakness towards temptation	27. Suicide
8. Forgetfulness	18. Financial Reverses	28. Self-hate
9. Tiredness	19. Pride	29. Frustration
10. Impatience	20. Anger	30. Depression.

5. Lord, cleanse my heart of all unforgiveness, resentment and bitterness.

6. Lord, help me to recognise the works and voice of the Holy Spirit.

7. I break myself loose from all ungodly subjection to any person living or dead in the name of Jesus.

8. I reject control or domination by any contrary spirit in Jesus' name.

9. Lord, forgive me if I have ever dominated or controlled some other persons in the wrong way.

10. I break all ties with evil associations whether conscious or unconscious in Jesus' name.

11. Lord, reveal to me every secret behind any problem that I have.

12. The Lord should make His Church and her members citadel of holiness, divine wonders and glory upon the earth.

13. God should bring the workers of His choice to His Church and keep others away.

14. I command all my buried blessings to be exhumed in Jesus' name.

15. Thank God for touching you in this session.

The love of ease is a strong enemy of prayer.

Scripture Reading: Numbers 23
Confession: Gal. 3:13,14

PRAYER POINTS

1. In the name of Jesus, I break any curse of rejection from the womb or illegitimacy which may be in my family back to ten generations on both sides of the family.
2. I renounce and break all evil demonic holds, strange powers, bondage and curses and loose myself and all my descendants from it.
3. I renounce and break all evil curses, charms, bewitchments put upon my family line and loose myself and all my descendants from them in Jesus' name.
4. I command every bad spirit of the curse to release me and go now.
5. Lord, unearth and destroy all buried spiritual items meant to do me harm.
6. I break any and all curses and send the spirits attached to them back to the sender in Jesus' name.
7. I return evil curses and send the spirits attached to them to the sender in Jesus' name.

Prayer is a love affair with God.

8. I loose myself from every dark spirit, evil influence and satanic bondage.
9. I take authority over and order the binding of every strongman in every department of my life.
10. I break every curse of automatic failure mechanism working in my family back to ten generations on both sides of my family in the name of Jesus.
11. I break all the curses of deformity, infirmity and sickness in my family back to ten generations on both sides of my family in the name of Jesus.
12. I break every curse of heart failure, heart attack, heart disease and blood diseases in the name of Jesus.
13. Father, send Your angels to break, cut and destroy all fetters, bands, chains, ties, and bonds of whatever sort the enemy has placed on me in the name of Jesus.
14. I break and renounce every conscious and unconscious evil association with lodge, religious system, cults and close friends in the name of Jesus.
15. Father in the name of Jesus, breathe into me and my family, the spirit of wisdom. knowledge, fear of the Lord, power, love, sound mind and peace.
16. Let any prison door hindering my blessing open to me on their own accord after the order of Peter.

POWER TO THE FAINT

Scripture Reading: Acts 2
Confession: Isa. 40:29-31

PRAYER POINTS

1. Thank God for His promise of power from above and power of the world to come.
2. I recover all the virtues stolen from me during the times of ignorance in the name of Jesus.
3. I refuse and reject the embrace of the magnetizers of destruction in Jesus' name.
4. Father, reveal unto me the secret of forces militating against my breakthrough in Jesus' name.
5. I break and loose myself from every unprogressive attachment to my place of birth in Jesus' name.
6. Father, let the anointing for spiritual breakthrough come upon my life in Jesus' name.
7. Holy Spirit, take control of my life in Jesus' name.
8. Lord, let power change hands in every department of my life to the hands of the Holy Spirit.
9. Father in the name of Jesus, baptize me with fire from above.

Prayer makes a history of wonders.

10. Father, make me a channel of spiritual blessings to others in Jesus' name.
11. Father, let Your word have free course and be glorified in me.
12. God should perfect what is lacking in my faith in Jesus' name.
13. Pray for the deepening of God's work in your spirit.
14. Holy Spirit, reveal Yourself to me.
15. Father, open my eyes and ears to receive wondrous things from above in Jesus' name.

20 FROM PROBLEMS TO PROMOTION

Scripture Reading: Genesis 39 - 41
Confession: Jer. 30:16,17

PRAYER POINTS

1. Let all my departed glory be restored in Jesus' name.
2. Let all my captured blessings be released in Jesus' name.
3. Let my blood reject the spirit of infirmity in Jesus' name.
4. All invisible evil followers should be scattered in Jesus' name.
5. Let God arise and all the forces of Pharaoh, Herods and Babylon scatter in Jesus' name.
6. I release my life from any spiritual cage in the name of Jesus.
7. Let liquid fire pour down on all spiritual thieves in Jesus' name.
8. I bind, plunder and render to naught every power of delegated oppressors in Jesus' name.
9. I arrest and paralyse every evil architect and evil construction within and around me in Jesus' name.
10. Let all attacks by evil night creatures be neutralized in Jesus' name.
11. Let every demonic tree harbouring hidden blessings release their captives in Jesus' name.
12. Every gathering held in the air, land, water and forest contrary to my life should be scattered in the name of Jesus.

Prayer is a trade to be learned.

13. Let all agents issuing word curses against me, fall after the order of Balaam.
14. All antagonistic relatives and in-laws should receive divine touch in Jesus' name.
15. Every effect of strange handshake, strange kiss, satanically inspired removal of clothing and properties, be nullified in Jesus' name.
16. Let divine promotion and miracles galore overshadow my life.

God sometimes compels us to pray hard for the best things.

STRENGTH FOR THE WEAK HANDS AND FEEBLE KNEES

Scripture Reading: Matthew 12:4-21
Confession: Heb. 12:12

PRAYER POINTS

1. Lord, grant that I avoid useless quarrels that tire and wound without achieving any results.
2. Lord, keep me from angry outburst that draw unholy attention which leaves one uselessly weakened.
3. Lord, grant that I live my days calmly and fully.
4. Lord, give me a hunger for purity and holiness.
5. Lord, grant me triumphant perseverance.
6. I reject the spirits of disappointment, disillusionment and despair.
7. Let every witchcraft burial receive divine ressurection.
8. You powers of the oppressors, begin to sit in the seat you constructed for me.
9. Let the fire of the Holy Ghost clean my root from spiritual filth.
10. Let all enemies in disguise be forced by God's angel to reveal their identity.
11. Father, I ask that You send Your angels to fire arrows at evil vessels warring against me.
12. I claim my divine promotion today in Jesus' name.

Lukewarmness in prayer is nauseating with God.

13. I command all stubborn pursuers to pursue themselves in the name of Jesus.
14. I bind every spirit of fear and storm of panic in Jesus' name.
15. You devourers, vanish from my labours in Jesus' name.
16. Thank the Lord for answered prayers.

There is a difference between faith in prayer and prayer in faith.

ANOINTING WITH FRESH OIL

Scripture Reading: Psalms 23 and 24
Confession: Psalm 92:10

PRAYER POINTS

1. Pray in the spirit for ten minutes.
2. Pray for a reversal of effects and power of demonic name-callings.
3. The promises of God will not fail upon my life in the name of Jesus.
4. I withdraw my picture from the demonic world and evil circulation in the name of Jesus.
5. I release myself today from every demonic trap in Jesus' name.
6. Every goodness of mine that has been spiritually swallowed should be released in Jesus' name.
7. I challenge every spiritual poison in my body with Holy Ghost fire and command their ejection in the name of Jesus.
8. I receive strength to do that which my enemies say is impossible in the name of Jesus.
9. Let every spirit of Judas in my camp be revealed in Jesus' name.
10. I decree confusion into the camp of the oppressors.
11. Lord, deliver me from any stronghold satan may have in my life because of my sins and those of my ancestors.
12. I break and lose myself from ungodly soul ties with all sex partners and unfriendly friends of the past in Jesus' name.

Prayer is the tongue of faith.

13. I reject every spirit of heaviness, slumber and paralysis in Jesus' name.
14. I command foreign strangers to depart from the house of my life in Jesus' name.
15. I ask You Father in the name of Jesus to send Your angels to cause to come into my treasury everything the devil has stolen from my life.
16. I command every power prolonging any battle in my life to receive permanent defeat in the name of Jesus.

Prayer converts promise into performance.

BE SHAKEN AND BE EMPTIED

Scripture Reading: Haggai 2
Confession: Haggai 2:6,7

PRAYER POINTS

1. Stand against the following things whether you are involved or not.
   (a) Poison in the body and blood
   (b) Invisible spiritual load
   (c) Wicked decisions
   (d) Stubborn pursuers
   (e) Spirit of marriage destruction
   (f) Satanic coffins
   (g) Evil spiritual deposits.
2. Lord, empty me of self and fill me with Your power.
3. Let all that has to be shaken out of my life be shaken in Jesus' name.
4. I release myself from problems associated with spiritual pad-locks.
5. I cancel and revoke all negative remote controlling and evil spiritual satellites in the name of Jesus.
6. I receive power to subdue all the oppressors in Jesus' name.

Prayer opened the red sea.

7. I refuse to wear any garment of shame in Jesus' name.
8. Let every thing that need to be shaken off by the Holy Spirit, be emptied out in the name of Jesus.
9. Let every thing that need to be emptied in my life by the Holy Spirit be emptied out in the name of Jesus.
10. All confiscated organs of the body stored in evil banks should be recovered and put back in the name of Jesus.
11. Let all problems that have their roots in the second heavens, on the earth and underneath the earth, receive divine solution in Jesus' name.
12. Let all troubles attached to serpentine spirits receive divine solution in the name of Jesus.
13. I stand against every faith destroyer in my life in Jesus' name.
14. Let any problem attached to my name or my family name, be neutralized in the name of Jesus.
15. I bind and paralyse every strongman attached to any specific problem that I have in the name of Jesus.
16. I refuse to become a spiritual dust-bin in the name of Jesus.
17. Every spiritual opposition to receiving breakthroughs in my spiritual life should be melted away by the fire of the Holy Spirit.
18. I withdraw the staff of office of any foreign king in my life in Jesus' name.
19. I withdraw all my properties in the possession of the strongman back in the name of Jesus.
20. Let the finger of God convert my rod into that which would swallow up the rods of Pharaoh's magicians in Jesus' name.
21. Thank God for a successful session.

Too many prayers are earthbound.

BUSINESS SUCCESS AND VICTORY OVER FINANCIAL DEVOURERS

Confession: Psalms 56:9; 32:8; 23:1,6, Exodus 23:20

PRAYER POINTS

1. Let all my enemies turn back because God is for me.
2. As you are turning back, let the doors of business opportunities open for me; morning, afternoon and evening.
3. Let profitable business meet me on the way in Jesus' name.
4. No devourer shall destroy the fruit of my labour in Jesus' name.
5. You devourers and wasters of fortune, I command you to depart from my life in the name of Jesus.
6. I use the Blood of Jesus Christ to wash my hands and my entire body and make them clean today.
7. I retrieve my blessings from every evil attack in Jesus' name.
8. I break every curse of failure in the name of Jesus.
9. Let the Lord reveal to me every secret behind the problem in my business.
10. I command the devil to take off his legs from any money that belongs to me in the name of Jesus.
11. Let the ministering spirits (God's Angels) go forth and bring in blessings unto me in the name of Jesus.
12. Let the rod of iron fall on any strange money passed to me in Jesus' name.

Prayer its the means through which God releases power.

 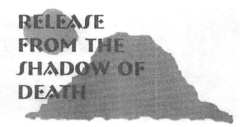

RELEASE FROM THE SHADOW OF DEATH

Confession: Psalms 23:4; 27:1-3; 118:17, Deut. 33:25-27, John 10:10, 2 Tim. 4:18, Phil. 4:13

PRAYER POINTS

1. Praise God because of the power of ressurection and life.
2. I release myself from every curse of untimely death in Jesus' name.
3. I break every unprofitable covenant regarding untimely death in the name of Jesus.
4. I remove my life from every shadow of death in Jesus' name.
5. I bind and paralyse every strongman of death and hell in Jesus' name.
6. Lord, strengthen my body, soul and spirit.
7. Let every secret concerning battles against my spiritual life be revealed in Jesus' name.
8. I reject and release myself from the grip of the spirit of infirmity.
9. I drink the blood of Jesus into the whole of my system.
10. Lord, build around me the hedge of fire.
11. Let the spirit of life replace the spirit of death in my life.
12. Woe unto the demonic vessel that the enemy would use to cause me spiritual injury.
13. Let Your glory cover every aspect of my life in Jesus' name.
14. Father, let Your Angels encamp around me in Jesus' name.

Prayer made the sun stand still.

ENJOYING MARITAL BLISS

Confession: Psalms 68:1; 24:1,22; 32:8, 1 Cor. 7:14, 1 John 4:4, Rev. 13:10, Josh. 11:5, Isa. 54:17; 50:7, Jer. 10:23; 1:8,9, Matt. 18:18, Prov. 21:1,2, Col. 1:9,10; 2:14,15, Job 5:12; 5:20; 22:28

PRAYER POINTS

1. I bind, plunder and render to naught every spirit militating against our family.
2. I command every stronghold rising up against my peace to be demolished in Jesus' name.
3. I drink the Blood of the Lord Jesus Christ.
4. Let the Fire of the Holy Ghost soak the whole of our house.
5. Let my environment and family situations become too hot for the devil to handle.
6. Holy Ghost, incubate me in Your Fire.
7. I disband all the host camping against our home in Jesus' name.
8. Let the Hand of the Lord be upon me for good in Jesus' name.
9. I bind every spirit of mind blindness in my husband/wife in Jesus' name.
10. I challenge every association gathered against our family with fire and lightning in Jesus' name.
11. I command every evil marriage covenant to break in Jesus' name.

Prayer brought fire down from heaven.

12. Let all marks of hatred put on me to disband our family be washed away by the Blood of Jesus.
13. I break the power of evil controlling spirits.
14. The Lord should reveal to me every secret behind this problem.

With Prayer, mountains shall move.

EXAMINATION SUCCESS

Scripture Reading: Psalms 19; 119:99, Daniel 1:17-20, 1 Kings 3:12, Exodus 31:2,3,6

Confession: Exodus 11:3, Psalms 34:7; 138:8, Acts 2:47; 4:13

PRAYER POINTS

1. I have more understanding than my teachers because God's testimonies are my meditations in Jesus' name.
2. Lord, give me understanding and wisdom.
3. I receive wisdom, knowledge and understanding for my studies.
4. Angels of the living God, encamp round about me now and go before me to lectures and examinations.
5. Father Lord, anoint me for success in my handiwork.
6. All questions directed at Daniel were answered, so I should have answers to questions in the examinations in the name of Jesus.
7. I excel over my colleagues ten times like Daniel in the name of Jesus.
8. I will find favour before all the examiners in the name of Jesus.
9. The Lord should perfect everything concerning my studies.
10. I bind and render to nothing every spirit of fear in the name of Jesus.
11. I release myself from every spirit of confusion and errors.

Prayer alters people on the inside.

12. Father Lord, lay Your hand of Fire upon my memory and give me retentive memory in the name of Jesus.
13. Lord, keep me diligent in my private preparations.
14. Lord, let me be very attentive to my lectures / lessons.
15. Father, I dedicate all my faculties to You in the name of Jesus.

RECEIVING FROM THE LORD

PRAYER POINTS

1. Repent from all known sins.
2. Find out scriptures that promise to you what you desire:
   Romans 8:32, Deut. 28:13, Isa. 41:11,12; 62:4, Psalm 91:13, Phil. 4:13, Joshua 1:5, Jer. 1:8,9, Prov. 16:7
3. Memorize and meditate on these scriptures and feed constantly on them promising you victory.
4. Quote these scriptures against satan, worry, anxiety, fear and negative circumstances.
5. Ask the Father in the name of Jesus for the desire of your heart. Believe that you have already received.
6. Resolve not to allow doubt to enter your mind. Reject every thought of failure, doubt. **REJECT** every dream, vision, prophecy that tells you that your prayers are not answered.
7. See yourself in the new position and keep confessing it.
8. Always give thanks to God for the answer to your prayers.

Pray out lies and pray in truth.

 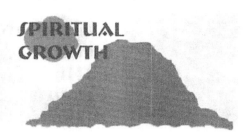

PRAYER POINTS

1. Father Lord, establish me in every good work.
2. Spirit of God, help me and increase me in the knowledge of God.
3. Lord, strengthen me with all might.
4. Lord, give me the eyes of understanding and enlighten me in the name of Jesus.
5. Father Lord, let Your Word have free course and be glorified in me.
6. Lord, let utterance be given unto me to make known Thy mystery of the Gospel.
7. God should perfect what is lacking in my faith in the name of Jesus.
8. Lord, make Your way plain before my face.
9. Let the Spirit of the Living God reveal my innermost being to me.
10. Lord, let Your glory shine upon me.
11. Pray for the deepening of God's work in your spirit.
12. Ask for the anointing to prosper in God's work.

Prayer is acting with God in this battle against evil.

RELEASE FROM INFIRMITY

Confession: Exodus 15:26; 23:25, Deut. 7:15, Psalms 34:19,20; 91:10; 103:1-4, Isa. 54:17; 53:5,6, Matt. 8:1-7, Mal. 4:2, Luke 10:19, Gal. 3:13,14, Rev. 12:1

PRAYER POINTS

1. Thank the Lord for your redemption.
2. Confess your sins before the Lord and ask for forgiveness.
3. Cover yourself with the Blood of Jesus.
4. Apply the Blood of Jesus to every part of your body.
5. Ask for the presence of the Holy Spirit.
6. I loose and release myself from the curse of infirmity in Jesus' name.
7. I denounce and renounce any covenant of sickness formed consciously or unconsciously whether by me or on my behalf in the name of Jesus.
8. I command the covenanted spirits of the curse and evil covenants to go in the name of Jesus.
9. You spirit of . . . *(mention the name of the sickness)*, loose your hold and depart from my body in the name of Jesus.
10. I release myself from every inherited sickness in the name of Jesus.

Prayer breaks down every opposing wall.

11. Lord, let the Power of the Holy Spirit overshadow me.
12. I command all hidden sicknesses to depart from my life in the name of Jesus.
13. Lord, perform the necessary surgical operation that would make me whole on my body.
14. Holy Ghost Fire, burn in every department of my body and destroy every satanic deposit.
15. I claim divine health in the name of Jesus.
16. I withdraw my name from the book of oppression in the name of Jesus.
17. I fire back every arrow of infirmity to the senders.
18. I shall not die but live to declare the works of God.
19. Let every desire and expectation of the enemy in my life come to naught.
20. My body will not be used as food by demons in the name of Jesus.
21. My body will not become a sacrifice on any demonic altar in Jesus' name.
22. My body will not be used as transport vehicles to demonic meetings in the name of Jesus.
23. I loose myself from any spell, hex, curse, bewitchment directed against my (a) head area; (b) chest area; (c) stomach area; (d) reproductive organs; (e) hands and legs in the name of Jesus.
24. Let every germ, parasite and poison working against my health be neutralized by God's Fire in the name of Jesus.
25. Lord Jesus, transfuse me with Your Blood.
26. Father, perform a creative miracle in every area of my body requiring such in the name of Jesus.
27. Thank the Lord for your healing.

Prayer demolishes every fortress of hell.

HEALING SCRIPTURES

1. **GENERAL** - *Psalms 30:2; 34:10; 34:19; 55:18; 97:10b; 103:3; 119:93, Isa. 53:4; 53:4, John 8:36, Romans 8:2; 8:32, 2Cor. 2:14, 1John 3:8, 3John 2, 1Peter 2:24.*

2. **ABDOMINAL** - *Psalm 30:2, Prov. 3:7,8; 4:20:22.*

3. **ARTHRITIS** - *Gal. 3:13,14, Job 4:3,4, Psalms 145:14; 146:7,8, Prov. 14:30; 16:24, Isa. 35:3, Heb. 12:12,13.*

4. **ASTHMA** - *Psalm 91:3, Lamentation 3:56, Joel 2:32, Acts 17:25b.*

5. **BLOOD DISEASES** - *Psalm 138:7, Prov. 3:5-8, Heb. 4:12, Ezek. 16:6b, Joel 3:21, 1Cor. 3:16.*

6. **BED WETTING** - *Psalms 25:20; 32:6b; 69:15; 144:7, Matt. 8:17b.*

7. **BONES** - *Psalms 6:2; 32:3; 34:20, Prov. 3:5-8; 14:30; 17:22, Isa. 58:11a, Heb. 4:12.*

8. **CANCER** - *Prov. 4:20-22, 2Tim. 1:7, 2Thessa. 3:3, Matt. 15:13, Mark 11:23,24.*

9. **DIABETES** - *Psl. 103:3; 107:20; 138, Prov. 12:18, Jer. 17:14a; 33:6, 1Pet. 3:12a, 3John 2, James 5:16.*

10. **EYES AND EARS** - *Psl. 146:8a, Isa. 29:18; 32:3; 35:5; 42:7, Matt. 11:5, Heb. 13:8, Job 36:15, Psalm 91:3.*

11. **FEVER** - *Matt. 8:17b, Luke 4:38b-39.*

12. **HEADACHES - MIGRAINES** - *Psalms 25:18; 42:11c; 119:25; 119:50, Isa. 57:19, John 14:27, Rom. 8:11.*

13. **HEART DISEASE** - *Psalms 27:14; 28:7; 31:24; 73:26, Prov. 4:23; 17:22.*

14. **SLEEPLESSNESS** - *Psalms 3:5; 4:8; 127:2, Prov. 3:24, Eccl. 5:12, Isa. 29:10.*

15. **PAIN** - *Psalms 25:18; 25:20; 147:3, Isa. 53:4, John 14:27.*

16. **STROKES** - *1Samuel 2:4, Psalms 56:12-13; 116:8-10; 138:7; 145:14, Prov. 3:23.*

Overloaded hearts are weak prayer warriors.

17. **POISONING** - *Mark 16:18*
18. **SPIRIT OF SLEEPINESS** - *Psalm 132:4, Prov. 20:13, Rom. 13:11.*
19. **TIREDNESS** - *Psalm 138:7, Isa. 40:29; 40:31, Matt. 8:17, Rom. 8:26, 1Cor. 6:17, 2Cor. 3:6.*
20. **ULCERS - WOUNDS** - *Psalm 147:3, Jer. 30:17.*
21. **HEARTACHE** - *Psalms 28:7; 34:18; 147:3, Prov. 4:23; 15:13, Isa. 30:15b, Jer. 31:13b.*

RELEASE OF CHILDREN FROM BONDAGE

Confession: Psalms 32:8; 127, Job 22:28, Col. 1:9,10, 1 Car. 7:14, Luke 1:37, 1 John 4:4, Isa. 8:10,18, Deut. 28:7, Rom. 16:20

PRAYER POINTS

1. I bind every spirit contrary to the spirit of God preventing me from enjoying my children.
2. I bind every spirit blinding their minds from receiving the glorious light of the Gospel of our Lord Jesus Christ.
3. Let all spirits of stubbornness, pride and disrespect for parents flee from their lives in the name of Jesus.
4. Father, destroy anything in my children preventing them from doing Your will in the name of Jesus.
5. Every curse, evil covenant and all inherited problems passed down to the children should be cancelled in the name of Jesus.
6. Mention their names one by one and tell the Lord what you want them to become.
7. Let every association and agreement between my children and my enemies be scattered in the name of Jesus.
8. My children will not become mis-directed arrows in Jesus' name.
9. I release my children from the bondage of any evil domination in the name of Jesus.

Prayers are deathless.

10. Let all evil influences by demonic friends clear away in Jesus' name.
11. You . . . *(mention the name of the child)*, I dissociate you from any conscious or unconscious demonic groupings or involvement in the name of Jesus.
12. I receive the mandate to release my children from the prison of any strongman in the name of Jesus.
13. Let God arise and all the enemies of my home be scattered.
14. Every evil influence and activity of strange women on my children should be nullified in the name of Jesus.

DELIVERANCE
FROM
DEMONIC SEXUAL
RELATIONSHIP

PRAYER POINTS

1. Father, I confess that, in the past, I had held unforgiveness, sometime bitterness and resentment in my heart against certain people who had hurt or disappointed me.

   I now recognise this as a sin and confess it as sin, for You have said in Your Word that if we confess our sin, You are faithful and just to forgive us our sin and to cleanse us of all unrighteousness (1John 1:9).

   I do now forgive the following people, whom I can remember, who have hurt or disappointed me. *(Mention names of those who come to your mind.)* I now freely forgive all these people and ask You to bless them if they are living. I also forgive myself for all my many faults and failures, for You have freely forgiven me.

   Thank You Father for freedom from the load of unforgiveness, bitterness and resentment in Jesus' name.

2. Father, I confess to You, that in the past, through ignorance, through curiosity or through wilfulness, I have come into contact with certain immoral acts. I now recognise this as sin and confess it as sin, claiming forgiveness in the name of Jesus.

   Specifically, I do confess as sin and renounce all contacts which I have had with the following immoral acts. *(Here, mention any*

The arm of God responds to violent prayers.

thing in this category with which you have dabbled or become involved e.g. fornication, abortion, watching immoral films, etc.)

3. I also renounce and confess as sin any oath which I have made to any false god and any idolatry in which I have been involved.

4. Satan, I rebuke you in the name of Jesus, and I am closing any door which I or my ancestors may have opened to you and your demons in the name of Jesus.

5. I renounce satan and all his demons, I declare them to be my enemies and I command them out of my life completely in the name of Jesus.

6. In the name of Jesus Christ, I now claim deliverance from any and all evil spirits which may be in me (Joel 2:28). Once and for all, I close the door in my life to all occult practices and command all related spirits to leave me now in the name of Jesus.

7. I break every curse of family destruction in the name of Jesus.

8. I release myself from the hold of any sexual strongman in the name of Jesus.

9. I command all spirit wives/husbands to loose their hold upon my life in the name of Jesus.

10. *Call the spirit you do not desire in your life by name. Then issue the command firmly and repeatedly that the spirits must come out in the name of the Lord Jesus.*

    Pray as follows: You spirit of . . . ,

    1) Lust *(all the sex spirits which entered through the eyes, ears participation, transfer or by inheritance)*

    2) Sex perversion of all kinds including oral sex

    3) Filthy conversations

    4) Filthy imaginations

    5) Condemnation   7) Shame   9) Homosexualit

    6) Guilt   8) Pornography   10) Lesbianism

The infinite resources of God are at the command of prayer.

11) Anal Sex	21) Prostitution	31) Succubi
12) Bestiality	22) Uncleanliness	32) Lasciviousness
13) Sadism	23) Filth	33) Lewdness
14) Masochism	24) Filthy dreams	34) Nudity
15) Adultery	25) Sexual fantasies	35) Promiscuity
16) Incest	26) Cruelty	36) Flirting
17) Rape	27) Frigidity	37) Seduction
18) Immorality	28) Lust of the eyes and lust of the flesh	38) Fornication
19) Occult sex	29) Incubi	39) Voyeurism
20) Harlotry	30) Impotence	40) Sexual Flashbacks

Come out of the sex organs, the lips, tongue, the taste buds, throat, and mind in the name of Jesus. *(Each of these things is backed by specific demon spirit. Do not lump everything together. Command each one to go out at a time. You must be specific if you have to be free.)*

11. I loose myself from you, in the name of Jesus and command you to leave me right now in the name of Jesus.

Pray always for the devil prays always.

VICTORY OVER SATANIC DREAMS

Confession: Obad. 1:3,4, Jer. 1:19, 1 John 4:4, 2 Tim. 4:18, Rev. 12:11, Isa. 54:17, Psalms 125:3; 91; 109:17

PRAYER POINTS

1. Praise worship.
2. I arrest every spiritual attacker and paralyse their activities in my life in the name of Jesus.
3. I retrieve my stolen virtues, goodness and blessings in Jesus' name.
4. Let all satanic manipulations through dreams be dissolved in Jesus' name.
5. Let all arrows, gunshots, wounds, harassment, opposition in dreams return to the sender in the name of Jesus.
6. I reject every evil spiritual load placed on me through dreams in Jesus' name.
7. All spiritual animals (cats, dogs, snakes, crocodiles, etc.) paraded against me should be chained and returned to the senders in the name of Jesus.
8. Holy Ghost, purge my intestine and my blood from satanic foods and injections.
9. I break every evil covenant and initiation through dreams in Jesus' name.

Why worry when you can pray?

10. I disband all the hosts of darkness set against me in the name of Jesus.

11. Every evil imagination and plan contrary to my life should fail woefully in the name of Jesus.

12. Every doorway and ladder to satanic invasion in my life should be abolished forever by the Blood of Jesus.

13. I loose myself from curses, hexes, spells, bewitchments and evil domination directed against me through dreams in the name of Jesus.

14. I command you ungodly powers, release me in the name of Jesus.

15. Let all past satanic defeats in the dream be converted to victory in the name of Jesus.

16. Let all test in the dream be converted to testimonies in Jesus' name.

17. Let all trials in the dream be converted to triumphs in Jesus' name.

18. Let all failures in the dream be converted to success in Jesus' name.

19. Let all scars in the dream be converted to stars in Jesus' name.

20. Let all bondage in the dream be converted to freedom in Jesus' name.

21. Let all losses in the dream be converted to gains in Jesus' name.

22. Let all opposition in the dream be converted to victory in Jesus' name.

23. Let all weaknesses in the dream be converted to strength in Jesus' name.

24. Let all negative in the dream be converted to positive in Jesus' name.

25. I release myself from every infirmity introduced into my life through dreams in the name of Jesus.

Pray till your joy is full.

26. Let all attempts by the enemy to deceive me through dreams fail woefully in the name of Jesus.
27. I reject evil spiritual husband, wife, children, marriage, engagement, trading, pursuit, ornament, money, friend, relative, etc. in the name of Jesus.
28. Lord Jesus, wash my spiritual eyes, ears and mouth with Your blood.
29. The God who answereth by fire should answer by fire whenever any spiritual attacker comes against me.
30. Lord Jesus, replace all satanic dreams with heavenly visions and divinely-inspired dreams.

EVIL MARKS

PRAYER POINTS

1. My life, my business, reject all evil marks in Jesus' name.
2. All traps set by the enemy to catch me, you traps, search for the enemies and catch them in Jesus' name.
3. All the effects of evil marks upon my physical life and spiritual life, be cancelled in Jesus' name.
4. All demonic animals sent to me by household enemies to come and do evil in my life, receive the Thunder judgement of God in Jesus' name.
5. All my spiritual properties which the household enemies sat upon, I withdraw you in the name of Jesus.
6. I reject all evil testimony of the household enemies in Jesus' name.
7. All evil spiritual soldiers assigned to monitor my life, I command you to receive spiritual blindness in Jesus' name.
8. Everything that has been removed from my body to do evil, I recover you and nullify your activities in Jesus' name.
9. You garment of shame, you are not my size, so receive the Fire of God in Jesus' name.
10. I bind every spirit of tail, and I claim the spirit of the head in Jesus' name.

Doubt is the grave of prayer, beware.

THE
ƒPIRIT OF
DEATH
AND HELL

PRAYER POINTS

1. I renounce and break every death covenant that I have formed or which anyone has formed on my behalf in Jesus' name.
2. I remove the control of my life from the hands of any dead person in Jesus' name.
3. I stand against every covenant of sudden death in the name of Jesus.
4. Every blessing of mine that has been buried under the ground or under any water, be released in Jesus' name.
5. I cancel my name from every death register in the name of Jesus.
6. I stand against every form of tragedy in Jesus' name.
7. Every grave cloth over my life, be removed in the name of Jesus.
8. All my potentials that have been destroyed, receive life in the name of Jesus.
9. I stand against all the powers that push a person to hell fire in the name of Jesus.
10. I cover my spirit, soul and body with the Blood of Jesus.

The double-minded will not receive anything in prayer.

PRAYER POINTS

1. I nullify all curses of failure in my life in Jesus' name.
2. I pull down every stronghold of failure in my life, in my marriage, in my business, both physically and spiritually in the name of Jesus.
3. Every pipeline of failure into my life, I command you to receive the Fire of God and be consumed in the name of Jesus.
4. Every spiritual barrier and limitation to success in my life, I command you to break into pieces in the name of Jesus.
5. Every inherited and self-made failure in my life, I command you to receive repairs in the name of Jesus.
6. Every seed of failure in my life, I command you to be consumed by the Fire of God in the name of Jesus.
7. Every area of my life that I have lost to failure, I command you to be restored in Jesus' name.
8. You spirit of failure, loose your grip over my life in the name of Jesus.
9. I refuse to register in the school of failure in the mighty name of our Lord Jesus Christ.
10. O Lord, let me not eneter the trap of failure.

Prayer is the key faith to unlock the door.

SPIRIT OF IMPOSSIBILITY

PRAYER POINTS

1. You root of impossibility that is in my life, be uprooted in Jesus' name.
2. Curse of impossibility, jump out of my life in the name of Jesus.
3. Every plan of impossibility in my life, be set to naught in Jesus' name.
4. In the name of Jesus, I will make it!
5. You impossibility, loose your position in my life, be fed with sorrow in the name of Jesus.
6. Spirit of impossibility, loose your position in my life in Jesus' name.
7. Let every mark of impossibility be rubbed off from every department of my life in the name of Jesus.
8. I destroy every demonic network working against me in the name of Jesus.
9. I paralyse the spirit of fear and doubt in the name of Jesus.
10. I withdraw my name from the register of impossibility in the name of Jesus.
11. I refuse the spirit of the tail and I claim the spirit of the head in the name of Jesus.

Oh, what needless pain . . . because you can't pray.

STRANGE EYES AND STRANGE LEGS

PRAYER POINTS

1. All strange eyes that are monitoring my life for evil, receive permanent blindness in Jesus' name.

2. All strange eyes working contrary to my life since these days, receive the Fire of God in the name of Jesus.

3. Strange and bad legs that have walked into my life, walk out in the name of Jesus.

4. Let all evil eyes transmitting my progress to the world of darkness receive blindness in the name of Jesus.

5. Let all strange legs operating in my business, marriage and prosperity flee in the name of Jesus.

6. I cause spiritual confusion to come upon every evil monitoring device in the name of Jesus.

7. I command all evil body parts to be repaired in Jesus name.

8. Let there be full restoration of what strange legs have walked into my life to destroy in the name of Jesus.

9. I close every door of my life against strange legs in the name of Jesus.

10. I cover my goodness, blessing and prosperity with the Blood of Jesus.

Don't give up, your miracle is on the way.

RETURN SPIRITUAL ARROWS TO THE SENDER

PRAYER POINTS

1. All spiritual evil arrows that have been fired into my life that is troubling me, I reject you and I command you to depart in Jesus' name.

2. All spiritual evil arrows that have been fired into my life, receive the Thunder of God and begin to come out of my life in Jesus' name.

3. All spiritual evil arrows presently in my life, loose your grip and hold upon my life, and I send you back to the sender in the name of Jesus.

4. No weapon that is being fired against me shall prosper in Jesus' name.

5. Lord, whenever my name is being mentioned for evil wherever my enemies are thinking of evil, let the Thunder Fire of God strike them and let them flee in seven ways before me in the name of Jesus.

6. I refuse to be a candidate for satanic arrows in the name of Jesus.

7. Let all the arrows of the oppressors go back to the oppressors in the name of Jesus.

8. Lord, repair any damaged done to my life by evil spiritual arrows in the name of Jesus.

Sweet hour of prayer!

POWER FROM ON HIGH

PRAYER POINTS

1. Lord, purge me from the sin of pride.
2. Father Lord, I reject every power that comes from beneath in the name of Jesus.
3. I renounce every unprofitable power in my life in the name of Jesus.
4. Father Lord, clothe me with the garment of fire in the name of Jesus.
5. Lord, let Your anointing soak me from my head to the sole of my feet in the name of Jesus.
6. Lord, let the wind of the Holy Spirit blow His fullness into my life in the name of Jesus.
7. Let the fire of the Holy Ghost incubate every department of area of my life.
8. Let a mighty portion of the anointing of the Holy Spirit fall upon me in the name of Jesus.
9. O Lord, clothe me with power from on high.

Ask, . . . you will receive.

FREEDOM FROM CAPTIVITY

PRAYER POINTS

1. Every captivity binding me right from the womb of my mother, break in Jesus' name.
2. Every captivity binding me from my youth, I curse you now, break in the name of Jesus.
3. I turn my head loose from every captivity in the name of Jesus.
4. Lord, I command every area of my life which the devil is holding in captivity to be loosed in the name of Jesus.
5. You evil spirits that are assigned against my life in heaven, on earth and under the earth, be bound in the name of Jesus.
6. Every captivity binding my heart, be bound in the name of Jesus.
7. I release myself from the hands of evil captivity in the name of Jesus.
8. I command every captivity fashioned against me to become captive in the name of Jesus.
9. I command every spirit of captivity to go and spirit of freedom to come in the name of Jesus.

Knock, . . . it shall be opened unto you.

BREAK DOWN THE STRONGHOLD OF THE ENEMY

PRAYER POINTS

1. Every builder of evil stronghold in my life, I command you to receive the spirit of confusion in Jesus' name.
2. Thunder Fire of God, dismantle the stronghold of the enemy from the foundation of my life, and I command you to break and receive the fire of God in the name of Jesus.
3. Every stronghold of the enemy from the foundation of my life, I command you to break and receive the fire of God in the name of Jesus.
4. Every spirit monitoring my progress, I command you to be bound and be blinded in the name of Jesus.
5. I break down every bad stronghold built by my own mouth and I cancel the effect in the name of Jesus.
6. Every blessing of mine (husband, wife, marriage, business, spiritual and physical breakthrough), that the devil has caged, I command you to receive the Fire of God in the name of Jesus. And let the blessings be released in Jesus' name.
7. All those searching for good husband and wife, let the husband and wife be released to them, and let every covenant of late marriage break in the name of Jesus.
8. All you carriers of heavy load, carry your loads in the name of Jesus.

Seek, . . . and you will find.

RELEASE FROM CURSES, COVENANTS, JINXES AND SPELLS

Confession: Gal. 3:13,14 & Col. 2:14,15

PRAYER POINTS

1. I break myself loose from every curse and unprofitable covenant in Jesus' name.
2. I release myself from the grip of every ancestral spirit in Jesus' name.
3. I fire back all spells and enchantments against me in Jesus' name.
4. Let the Blood of Jesus Christ wash my name away from the notebook of dark powers.
5. Let every evil attachment to my place of birth be disrupted in Jesus' name.
6. I pull out any organ from my body stored in satanic banks in Jesus' name.
7. Let every evil satanic eye observing my goodness be blinded in Jesus' name.
8. Lord, place me on the mountain of fire and miracles.
9. I break every curse of family destruction in Jesus' name.
10. I cancel and nullify any future covenant made against my life in the name of Jesus.
11. I cancel every evil effect of curses and covenants in Jesus' name.

Prayerless Christian is a powerless Christian.

EVIL MARKS (2)

Confession: Gal. 3:13,14

PRAYER POINTS

1. Let the precious Blood of Jesus cleanse my body from all marks of wizards.
2. Let the precious Blood of Jesus cleanse my body from all marks of witches.
3. Let the precious Blood of Jesus cleanse my body from all marks of familiar spirits.
4. Let the precious Blood of Jesus cleanse my body from all evil marks.
5. Angels of the Living God should remove filthy garments from me.
6. Lord, put on me the garment of honour.
7. Let the writers of evil mark in my life be bound and set on fire in the name of Jesus.

If you pray, you will do exploits.

DEFEATING HOUSEHOLD ENEMIES

Confession: Psalm 16:8, Micah 7:6, Matt. 10:36

PRAYER POINTS

1. Turn me to hot coals of untouchable fire.
2. Reveal unto me every spiritual parasite.
3. I break every demonic family hold.
4. I bind every ancestral spirit in the name of Jesus.
5. Lord, let Your Fire melt away every spiritual deposit planted by intimate enemies in my life in the name of Jesus.
6. I bind all suckers of peace.
7. I bind all suckers of happiness.
8. I retrieve my blood from every evil altar.
9. I retrieve any material from my body from every evil altar.
10. I loose myself from any linkage to any family idol-generation behind.
11. I retrieve all my blessings from the hands of household enemies.
12. I retrieve all my prosperity from the hands of household enemies.
13. I retrieve all my children from the hands of household enemies.
14. I retrieve my home from the hands of household enemies.

If you don't pray, you will be exploited.

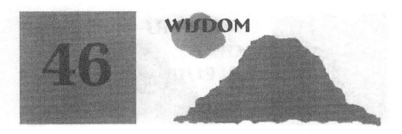

WISDOM

46

Confession: Psalm 119:99

PRAYER POINTS

1. The Lord should open up my understanding.
2. Ask for the spirit of wisdom.
3. Ask for the spirit of revelation.
4. Ask for the spirit of knowledge.
5. Revive my beneficial potentials.
6. Lord, remember me for good.
7. Lord, teach me deep and secret things.
8. Remove my name from the book of failure.
9. Let Holy Ghost Fire dry up all memory failure.

How many problems has worry and anxiety solved?

SHOWERS OF BLESSING

PRAYER POINTS

1. Command the devil to take his legs off any money that belongs to you.
2. I must eat the fruit of my labour in the name of Jesus.
3. Lord, open up the pipeline of prosperity into my business.
4. Silence and paralyse all devourers.
5. I bind the spirit of financial failure.
6. I loose the spirit of prosperity upon my life.
7. Ask for the anointing to prosper.
8. Let the rod of iron fall on any strange money passed to me.
9. I declare this year as a year of abundance.

Therefore, pray now!

BREAKTHROUGHS

Confession: Exodus 15:9-12

PRAYER POINTS

1. Speak fear into the camp of the enemy.
2. The anointing that destroys stubborn yokes should fall upon me.
3. Lord, cleanse me from every filthiness of the spirit.
4. The prayer of Moses - "Lord show me Your glory".
5. Holy Spirit, move in my life always.
6. Ask for breakthroughs -
   Financial
   Spiritual
   Marital
   Business
7. All strange altars should be broken in pieces.

Prayer of the righteous avails much.

Scripture Reading: Exodus 14:21, Job 27:20-23, Psalms 48:7; 78:26, Jer. 1:8, Eze. 19:12, Jonah 4:8
Confession: Psalm 75:6

PRAYER POINTS

1. The Lord should promote me from minimum to maximum.
2. I reject promotion from the East, West, South and the North, but I claim God's promotion in the name of Jesus.
3. Every hindrance to my physical and spiritual promotion should be removed.
4. Let the east wind blow away hindrances to my prosperity.
5. I loose myself from every evil spiritual attachment.
6. Let the Angels of God disband evil hosts around me.

PRAYER POINTS

1. Oh God, set my spirit on Fire of the Holy Ghost.
2. Oh God, fuel me to the brim with Your Power.
3. I bind the spirit of lukewarmness in the name of Jesus.
4. I bind the spirit of laziness in the name of Jesus.
5. Ask for the spiritual gifts.
6. I bind the spirit of pride.
7. Let Your Hand of Fire incubate me.
8. I bind the spirit of heaviness.
9. Ask the Lord to open your spiritual eyes and ears.

51 TREADING UPON

PRAYER POINTS

1. Ask for the power of anointing upon the host of hell all the time.
2. Ask for the power to reject evil arrows.
3. Ask for the power to keep your eyes on the Lord's table.
4. Lord, transfuse me with the Blood of Jesus.
5. Any spiritual invitation to oppressors in my body should depart.
6. Lord, wash me with Your spiritual sponge.
7. Let the Power of God shake off all evil spiritual attachments.
8. Let Your light shine on all my ways.

If the devil cannot win you on your knees, he cannot win you in any other way.

 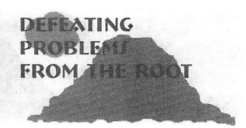

DEFEATING PROBLEMS FROM THE ROOT

52

PRAYER POINTS

1. O Lord, send Your Fire to the root of my life to dissolve any deeply rooted problem in my life in the name of Jesus.
2. I reject any curse flowing down to me from my ancestors in the name of Jesus.
3. I reject every inherited problem in the name of Jesus.
4. Every unconscious curse or playful curse that my parents have issued on me, I cancel it in the name of Jesus.
5. Let the secrets of every hidden stranger in my life be revealed in Jesus' name.
6. Any evil thing running in my family, run away from me in Jesus' name.
7. I wash the root of my life with the Blood of Jesus.

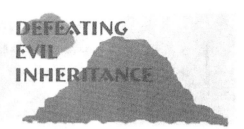

DEFEATING EVIL INHERITANCE

PRAYER POINTS

1. I refuse to inherit any evil load from my ancestors in Jesus' name.
2. I reject every evil Blood transfusion in the name of Jesus.
3. I cut off every evil communication link with dead, ungodly relatives in the name of Jesus.
4. I refuse to enter into the valley of failure designed for me through inheritance in Jesus' name.
5. Lord Jesus, wash away with Your Blood the repercussion of any unclean money spent on me by my parents.
6. I reject every evil inheritance; I claim divine blessings in Jesus' name.
7. You the strongman of my ancestors, release my blessings in your hands in the name of Jesus.

54

BODY FUNCTIONS

PRAYER POINTS

1. You camp of sickness fashioned against me, be destroyed. You cannot camp against me in the name of Jesus.
2. You curse of sickness, I command you to break in the name of Jesus.
3. Every bondage of sickness, break in Jesus' name.
4. You spirit of infirmity, depart from my life in the name of Jesus.
5. Oh Lord, wash me in Your Blood from the top of my head to the soles of my feet in Jesus' name.
6. I charge my body with the Fire of the Holy Ghost in the name of Jesus.
7. My body, shake off every arrow in the name of Jesus.
8. Every evil design for me, be cancelled in the name of Jesus.

"Give me this mountain O Lord."

PRAYERS FOR HOME

PRAYER POINTS

1. O Lord, let my household be covered by the Blood of Jesus.
2. Every stronghold of the enemies in my life, I command you to be dismantled in Jesus' name.
3. I bind every spirit of disunity in my home in the name of Jesus.
4. You demonic walls built against my spiritual life, melt away with the Fire of the Holy Ghost in the name of Jesus.
5. Every sickness in my body, soul and spirit, I command the ground to open up and swallow you all in the name of Jesus *(name the particular sickness)*.
6. Every load that God did not place on my head, I send you back to the sender in Jesus' name.

"Oh that Thou wouldest rend the heavens O Lord."

PRAYER POINTS

1. Every evil house that has my name there, let the Fire of God begin to cause havoc there in the name of Jesus.

2. Any part of my spirit that has been summoned by the devil, I command that part to receive healing in Jesus' name.

3. Every unprofitable oath made consciously or unconsciously that is negatively affecting my life, break in the name of Jesus.

4. You evil soul trader, release your captive in the name of Jesus.

5. You evil soul trader, release me in the name of Jesus.

6. Let every fragmented soul be gathered together now in the name of Jesus.

7. O Lord, restore my body, soul and spirit to the original one meant for me in the name of Jesus.

8. O Lord, let the Fire of God begin to cause havoc to any evil gathering or association affecting my life, break in the name of Jesus.

9. I receive strength through the Blood of Jesus.

57

SPIRIT OF COMPROMISE

PRAYER POINTS

1. I refuse to negotiate with any problem in my life in Jesus' name.
2. I refuse to negotiate with sickness/infirmity in my life in Jesus' name.
3. I refuse to negotiate with any force of the wasters in my life in the name of Jesus.
4. I refuse to negotiate with failure in my life in the name of Jesus.
5. Lord, visit me in a new way.
6. Lord, lead me to the top of the mountain when I am tired.
7. Lord, that which is pulling me down, I remove it in Jesus' name.
8. Wonderful Lord, I reverse any defeat that I have ever suffered in the dream in the name of Jesus.
9. O Lord, don't let me be a bad example in the name of Jesus.
10. O Lord, help me to be a victor and not to die at the battle front in the name of Jesus.
11. All you powers of the emptier, I curse you to be emptied in the name of Jesus.
12. Any dream that I have dreamt that is good and for God, I receive it, and those that are satanic, I reject them in the name of Jesus.

Pray more for there are "princes of Persia" in operation.

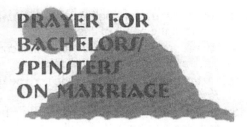

PRAYER FOR BACHELORS/ SPINSTERS ON MARRIAGE

Confession: Gen. 2:18, John 15:7, Prov. 18:22, Rom. 8:34, 1 Pet. 5:7, Col. 2:14,15, Phil. 4:19

PRAYER POINTS

1. Lord, I thank You because You care for me and my life is in Your hand.
2. Let the Power of the Holy Ghost magnetize my God-chosen partner to me in the name of Jesus.
3. I command all evil anti-marriage marks to be removed in the name of Jesus.
4. I break all evil covenants of false and late marriage in the name of Jesus.
5. I cancel every conscious and unconscious spiritual marriage in the name of Jesus.
6. Lord, open my spiritual eyes and ears to receive divine revelation concerning my life-partner.
7. Lord, show me the secrets of any marriage problem that I have.
8. Let every hindrance to a happy marital life be removed in the name of Jesus.
9. I return or cancel any spiritual bride-price paid or received on my behalf in the name of Jesus.

Who is bigger - is it God or the problem? Then pray.

10. Father, send Your Angels to link me up with Your chosen partner for me in the name of Jesus.

11. I break any anti-marriage generation curse backward to twenty generations in the name of Jesus.

12. Let the beauty and glory of the Lord be upon me in the name of Jesus.

13. I break every curse brought upon me by inherited sexual sins and also by personal sexual sins in the name of Jesus.

14. I bind every spirit of fear in the name of Jesus.

15. I renounce and break all anti-marriage covenants made by me or on my behalf in the name of Jesus.

16. I reverse every backwardness that worry has created in my life in the name of Jesus.

17. I cancel every anti-marriage spell, bewitchment and enchantment in the name of Jesus.

18. Let my partner and myself be for signs and wonders amongst the nations in the name of Jesus.

19. I bind the spirit of error and uncertainty in my life and the life of my partner in the name of Jesus.

20. Father Lord, reveal unto me Your choice for my life.

21. Let all rough places concerning this matter be made plain in the name of Jesus.

22. Stand against or break loose from:

    (a) spirit of marriage destruction

    (b) spirit of fear

    (c) anti-marriage covenant

    (d) spirit husbands/wives

    (e) inherited spirits

    (f) sales of sexual birth-right

Reject the tail violently and claim the head in prayer.

(g) spirit of frustration.

23. Let every blockage towards the manifestation of my miracle crumble in the name of Jesus.

BREAKING ANTI-MARRIAGE CURSES AND COVENANTS

Confessions: Col. 2:14,15; 1:13,14, Gal. 3:13,14, 2 Tim. 4:18, Isa. 53:3-5; 54:17, Rev. 12:11

PRAYER POINTS

1. Thank the Lord for His redemptive power which never fails nor diminish.
2. Ask the Lord to forgive your sins.
3. I break myself loose from every covenant of late or useless marriage in the mighty name of Jesus.
4. I release myself from every marital, ancestral curse in the name of Jesus.
5. I renounce and break all evil curses and bewitchment put upon my marriage in the mighty hands of our Lord Jesus Christ.
6. I take authority over and bind the strongman attached to the marriage department of my life in the name of Jesus.
7. I break all marital curses placed on me by household enemies in the name of Jesus.
8. I break all marital curses placed upon my life through witchcraft in the name of Jesus.
9. I command all demon spirits connected to the curse to release me and go now in the name of Jesus.

Prayer opens the heaven.

10. The Lord should reveal my life-partner to me during this prayer session.
11. Anything present in me that is anti-marriage in nature should go now in the mighty name of Jesus.
12. I break and release myself from every anti-marriage curse in Jesus' name
13. Let my would-be husband\wife be released to me by any evil power trying to hold back in the name of Jesus.
14. I cancel and revoke any spiritual marriage or childbirth contrary to the will of God in Jesus' name.
15. Let all family idols from both sides of my parents release me and my marital life in the name of Jesus.
16. I bind every strongman from my father's and mother's sides attached to my marital life.
17. I refuse to follow any evil pattern laid down or programmed by any of my ancestor in the name of Jesus.
18. I reject all ancestral burdens and bondage in Jesus' name.
19. I stand against:
    (a) demonic wedding rings
    (b) demonic wedding gowns/attire
    (c) spiritual trading of marriage or something else
    (d) evil spiritual marriage
    (e) instituted and remotely programmed frustration
    (f) anti-marriage habits and imaginations
    (g) fear of abandonment and loneliness
    (h) attraction to me by wrong and unserious partners
    (i) unprofitable impatience in the mighty name of Jesus.
20. Let all the veil hindering me from seeing what I should see be roasted by the fire of God in Jesus' name.
21. I release myself from all anti-marriage curses, spells, bewitchment, hexes, covenants operating on both sides of my family in Jesus' name.

Pursue, overtake and recover.

22. Let divine marital prosperity replace all the anti-marriage curses and covenants in the name of Jesus.

Please Note The Following:

1. You must repent from all sins;
2. If you have trouble with your dreams, seek for deliverance ministration or minister self-deliverance to yourself;
3. Ensure that all restitutions have been made;
4. Ensure that you are completely emptied of pride and anger;
5. Stop all forms of crying;
6. Memorize and read your Bible daily; and
7. Seek for the genuine baptism of the Holy Spirit.

SAFEGUARDING YOUR HOME AND RECONCILIATION

Confessions: Mark 10:8,9, Psl. 145:16, Col. 3:18,19, 1 Cor. 7:14,15, Isa. 43:18,19, Psl. 68:1, Job 22:28

PRAYER POINTS

1. Thank the Lord for His mercies and grace.
2. Ask the Holy Spirit to help you pray to the point of breakthrough.
3. *(Gird up your spiritual loins and aggressively stand against the following local home-wreckers. Pray as follows:)* I stand against any . . . , (fix in the items listed hereunder i.e. a-m) and command them to release me and my marriage in the name of Jesus.

   (a) Competition by strange women or girls\men
   (b) Demonic in-laws
   (c) Financial failure and poverty, especially after the wedding
   (d) Spirit husbands and wives
   (e) Demonic marks
   (f) Anti-marriage destruction
   (g) Spirit of fear
   (h) Spirit of Jezebel (domineering nature)
   (i) Inherited spirit from the father's and mother's sides
   (j) Marriage curses
   (k) Anti-marriage covenants

Impossibility is outside God's dictionary.

(l) Spirit of misunderstanding, misinterpretation and exaggeration
(m) Ungodly attachment to parents.

4. *(Cancel the effects of the following things. Please pray aggressively in your prayers if you are involved or feel you may be involved in them. Pray as follows:)* I cancel the satanic influence of . . . upon my marriage; I bind the connected spirits and command them to loose their hold upon my marriage in the name of Jesus.

(a) Demonic water pouring on legs on wedding day
(b) Contaminated wedding rings and shoes
(c) Background of polygamy and multiple husbands
(d) Familiar spirits and witchcraft spirits
(e) Satanic deposits in home
(f) Collection of spiritual bride-price
(g) Incest.

5. I break and loose myself from any anti-marriage curse issued upon my family in the name of Jesus.

6. Father, let the Prince of Peace reign in my marriage without any hindrance in Jesus' name.

7. I decree reconciliation between myself and my partner in the name of Jesus.

8. All powers conspiring with anyone to destroy our home\marriage should loose their hold in the name of Jesus.

9. All evil counsels against our home should be frustrated in the name of Jesus.

61 PRAYERS FOR ENGAGED PARTNERS PLANNING MARRIAGE

Praise Worship: "How Great Thou Art . . ."
Confession: Psalm 138:8, Philippians 1:6, 2 Tim. 1:7, Col. 2:14,15, Psalm 71:21, Zech. 4:7-9, Deut. 33:26,27

PRAYER POINTS

1. Thank God for His miraculous hand upon your life.
2. Confess every sin of unforgiveness, bitterness, anxiety, wrong thinking and forgive any who might have hurt or disappointed you.
3. I renounce, break and loose myself from every ancestral marital curse or bondage in Jesus' name.
4. I reject and refuse to follow any evil marriage pattern in Jesus' name.
5. Father, I ask You in the name of Jesus Christ to send out Your angels to all the corners of the earth on my behalf, and let them bring to me the favour, provisions, blessings and materials needed for a successful marriage.
6. I bind, plunder and render to naught every spirit of marriage destruction in Jesus' name.
7. Lord, unite those that would bless me and keep all others away.

The mighty men in the Bible were prayer addicts.

8. Let Your Holy Angels surround us. Let Your wall of fire be built around us. Let the Blood of Jesus cover us throughout every stage of the marriage.
9. All evil touch and evil arrows are completely neutralized in Jesus' name.
10. Father, let the spirit of joy, liberty, grace and love fill us to the brim.
11. Lord, give me power to avoid useless quarrels that tire and wound without achieving results.
12. Lord, give me power over angry outbursts that achieve nothing.
13. Lord, convert all the retreats that I have suffered into advances.
14. Lord, convert all my trials and tests to testimonies and triumph.

Behold, I am the LORD, the God of all flesh: is there any thing too hard for me?

Anger is a great spiritual sin and robber. Anger has incapacitated many useful lives. Read these scriptures and pray aggressively.

Job 5:2, Psl. 18:48, Prov. 16:32; 25:28; 29:22, Eccl. 7:9, Eph. 4:27; 4:31

PRAYER POINTS

1. Thank God for Calvary.
2. Ask the Lord to forgive you for every fit of anger you have allowed.
3. Holy Spirit, help me to crucify my flesh in Jesus' name.
4. Let all the works of the flesh be dismantled in my life in Jesus' name.
5. Lord, give me grace to overcome every iota of fear, pride and selfishness in my life.
6. I bind, plunder and render to naught every spirit of anger.
7. O Lord, help me to repair all the good altars that anger has broken down in my life.
8. Lord, emancipate me from the works of the flesh.
9. All evil desires and lust should be crucified in Jesus' name.
10. Lord, help me to develop and manifest the fruit of the spirit.

For with God nothing shall be impossible.

11 Lord, help me to put off anger or loss of temper and put on being tenderhearted.

12. Lord, help me to be quick to listen, slow to speak and dead to anger.

13. Father, give me the power to violently resist the devil so that he will flee from me.

14. Lord, help me to hear the voice of the Holy Spirit whenever I am being provoked and make me unprovokeable.

15. Lord, create in me a new heart by Your Power.

16. Lord, renew a right spirit within me.

17. I renounce my rights to anger.

18. Lord, remove from me the root of irritation that keeps anger alive in me.

19. I reject the thought that I will never change in the name of Jesus.

20. Spirit of God, cleanse and control anger in my life.

21. Lord, reduce in me the power of self-control and increase gentleness.

22. I reject all that robs me of the joy of my inheritance in Your kingdom.

23. I pseak to evil mountain and break their power over my life in the name of Jesus.

24. Lord, enable me to hear Your voice.

25. Lord, by the Power of the Blood, remove from my life any hindrance to my breakthroughs.

26. Lord, drive away all darkness in my life.

27. Lord, shield me from deception.

28. Lord, illuminate Your truth to my understanding.

29. Lord, let me with the eyes of my heart see You more clearly.

The things which are impossible with men are possible with God.

DEFEAT THE SPIRIT OF FEAR

Fear is a strongman. It is one of the powerful ways in which satan controls mankind. Make the confession regularly and pray constantly. (Obtain a copy of our booklet: "Students In The School of Fear".)

Deut. 31:8, Psl. 23:4; 27:1; 34:4; 56:11; 91:5, Isa. 41:10, Rom. 8:15, 2 Tim. 1:7, I John 4:18.

PRAYER POINTS

1. I bind and paralyse every strongman of fear in my life in the mighty name of Jesus.
2. I loose myself from the bondage of fear in the name of Jesus.
3. I loose myself from all negative religious fears, bondage to traditions of demons and men, religious images and witchcraft prophets in Jesus' name.
4. I loose myself from all demonic fears and release myself from all its tormenting and enslaving powers in the name of Jesus.
5. I loose myself from every unholy fear of man and I receive holy boldness, faith, confidence and inner strength in the name of Jesus.
6. Let all the doorways and entrances of fear in my life be closed forever in the name of Jesus.
7. I plead the Blood of Jesus over my heart, soul, spirit and body.
8. Let all the habitation of fear in my life be demolished in Jesus' name.

But Jesus behind them, and ssaid unto them, With men this is impossible; but with God all things are possible.

9. I bind every spirit of fear afflicting my life in the name of Jesus.

10. I render you spirit of fear of . . . *(name them)* powerless in the name of Jesus.

11. I expel every spirit of fear and I desire them out in the name of Jesus.

12. O Lord, break the bands of fear in my life.

13. Let all fears emanating from parental influence, past association and guilt depart from my spirit in Jesus' name.

14. I command the strongholds of fear to break in Jesus' name.

15. You spirit of fear, I command you to come out of your hiding places; depart from my mind, my emotions, my will, my spirit and my body in the name of Jesus.

16. Let all the problems introduced by fear into my life depart now in the name of Jesus.

17. Stand against the spirit of fear of:

- Airplanes	- Ambulances	- Failure	- Barbers	
- Other's opinion	- Future	- Heights	- Flying	
- Cats	- Chicken	- People	- Spiders	
- Cancer	- Heart disease	- Dogs	- Water	
- Demons	- Insects	- Marriage	- Women	
- Robbers	- Worms	- Blood	- Sleep	
- Skin diseases	- Ridicule	- Mice	- Corpses	
- Pregnancy	- Insanity	- Disease	- Crowds	
- Children	- Poverty	- Dreams	- Ghosts	
- Rivers	- Fire	- Satan	- Speed	- Being Alone
- Death	- Poison	- Animals	- Being stared at	
- Childbirth	- Number 13	- Darkness	- Sexual Intercourse	

in the name of Jesus.

Only believe.

DELIVERANCE AND BREAKTHROUGH PRAYERS FOR INSTITUTIONS AND BUSINESS

Confession: Gen. 39:3, Deut. 28:3-13, Josh. 1:8, II Chron. 20:20, Neh. 2:19,20, Psl. 55:11, Phil. 4:19.

PRAYER POINTS

1. In Jesus' name, I ask the Father for sufficient legions of the Holy Angels to bind all satanic forces in my institution/business and in the air overhead, so they will be unable to interfere into my institution/business again.

2. I take authority over and order the binding of the strongman of financial failure.

3. I command the curse and ordination of debt in my life and institution/business to be nullified in Jesus' name.

4. Lord, anoint my brain to prosper after the order of Bazaleel, the son of Uri, the son of Hui, of the tribe of Judah.

5. Let the anointing of fire be in all my writings, thinking and organisation.

6. I stamp out every spirit of anger, lack of co-operation, wrong judgements, contentions and disloyalty amongst staff in Jesus' name.

7. Let my life and this institution/business become a channel of blessings and a foundation of life for other lives and institution/business in Jesus' name.

Is it barrenness? Remember Sarah at 90 (Gen. 18:11).

8. Let the showers of financial revival fall upon my life and my institution/business.

9. Lord, anoint all letters emanating from us for help to go forth accompanied by divine favour, angelic transportation and positive results.

10. I reverse all word curses that have been issued against my life and my institution/business in Jesus' name.

Is it curse? Remember the cross - Gal. 3:13,14.

65

RELEASE OF PROSPERITY ON BUSINESS AND BUSINESS TRANSACTIONS

Confession: Deut. 3:19; 31:66, Psalm 46:1,5; 68:19; 35:27b; 24:1, Jer. 32:27, Phil. 4:19, III John 2, I Sam. 30:8, Job 22:28, Matt. 7:7

Confess this modified version of Psalm 23.

The Lord is my banker ;I shall not owe. He maketh me to lie down in green pastures; He restoreth my loss: He leadeth me beside still waters. Yea though I walk in the valley of the shadow of debt, I will fear no evil, for thou art with me; thy silver and thy gold, they rescue me. Thou preparest a way for me in the presence of business competitors; Thou anointed my head with oil, my cup runneth over. Surely goodness and mercy shall follow me all the days of my life and I shall do business in the name of the Lord. Amen

PRAYER POINTS

1. Let there be a breakthrough for me in my transactions in the name of Jesus.
2. Lord, let me have the spirit of favour in this business transaction.
3. I ask for the release of prosperity on my business in Jesus' name.
4. Let all demonic hindrances to my finances be totally paralysed.
5. I break every circle of failure in Jesus' name.
6. Let my business be shielded away from all evil observers in the name of Jesus.

Is it fear? Remember 2 Tim. 1:7.

7. I claim all my blessings in the name of Jesus.
8. Let all business problems receive divine solution in Jesus' name.
9. Let men go out of their ways to show favour unto me in the name of Jesus.
10. Lord, let not the lot of the wicked fall upon my business.

RELEAJE OF (I) LOJT AND JTOLEN ITEMJ (II) DEBTJ AND (III) UNLAWFULLY CONFIJCATED PROPERTIEJ

Confession: I Sam. 30:8, Psalm 18:37; 126:1, Exod. 3:20, Isa. 45:13, Phil. 4:19, Rom. 8:31,32; 8:37; 9:33

PRAYER POINTS

1. I recover all my confiscated and stolen properties in Jesus' name.
2. You devil, take off your legs from my . . . in Jesus' name.
3. I bind every strongman holding my privileges and rights captive in Jesus' name.
4. I retrieve any of my properties from the satanic banks in Jesus' name.
5. Let the angels of God ordain terrifying noises to chase out all stubborn and uncooperative occupants.
6. I possess all my possessions in the name of Jesus.
7. Lord, restore seven-fold everything that spiritual thieves have stolen from me.
8. I bind every spirit operating to keep my possession occupied and keeping me away from taking full charge.
9. Lord, make all my properties too hot for the enemy to sit upon.
10. *(Now be specific, quoting the preceding scriptures.)*

It is finished, said Jesus on the cross.

RELEASE OF FUNDS INTO BUSINESS

Confession: Deut. 8:18, 3 John 2, Job 36:11, Col. 2:14,15, Ps. 84:11; 24, Phil. 4:13

PRAYER POINTS

1. Let the spirit of favour be opened upon me everywhere I go concerning my business.
2. Father, I ask You in the name of Jesus to send ministering spirits to bring in prosperity and funds into my business.
3. Let men bless me anywhere I go.
4. I release my business from the clutches of financial hunger in the name of Jesus.
5. I loose angels in the mighty name of Jesus to go and create favour for my company.
6. I bind the spirit in all of the staff members who will try to use evil weapons against me, including lying, gossip, slander and opinionated spirits.
7. Let all financial hindrances be removed in Jesus' name.
8. I remove my name and those of my customers from the book of financial bankruptcy.
9. Holy Spirit, be the Senior Partner in my business.
10. Every good thing presently eluding my business should flow into it in the mighty name of Jesus.

11. I reject every spirit of financial embarrassment in the name of Jesus.
12. Father, block every space causing unprofitable leakage to my company in the mighty name of Jesus.
13. Let my company become too hot to handle for dupes and demonic customers.
14. Let spiritual magnetic power that attracts and keeps wealth be deposited in my company in the name of Jesus.

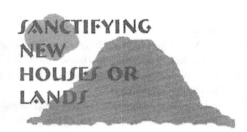

68 SANCTIFYING NEW HOUSES OR LANDS

Obtain a copy of the message: "Deliverance For Inanimate Objects" and use it alongside the prayers.
Confession: Zech. 2:5

PRAYER POINTS

1. Father, please send Your angels to be 24 hours daily round this compound in Jesus' name.
2. I soak every grain of sand that forms part of the soil of this compound in the Blood of Jesus.
3. Let the foundation, the roof and the walls of this house be covered with the wonderful Blood of Jesus.
4. I dislodge and bind every evil mixture in the concrete of this house in Jesus' name.
5. Father, send Your angels to exhume any property of the evil one that may have been buried in the ground of this compound and make a bonfire of them in Jesus' name.
6. Blood of Jesus, fall like showers upon this compound.
7. Holy Ghost Fire, incubate and take full control of this environment.
8. I cancel any curse that must have been uttered against this compound and its contents with the Blood of Jesus and I loose this compound from its power in Jesus' name.

And give him no rest, till he establish, and till he make Jerusalem a praise in the earth.

9. Let any evil remote control wave directed towards this compound be roasted in Jesus' name.
10. Father, let the blessings of heaven fall like rain upon this house and its occupants in Jesus' name.
11. I cancel every conscious or unconscious curse uttered by unhappy construction workers in Jesus' name.
12. Pray a "wall of fire" around the land or house.

Just a closer walk with Jesus in prayer will clear it all.

POWER AGAINST PROBLEMS WITH REPRODUCTIVE ORGANS

Praise Worship
Confession: Psalm 56:9, Rom. 16:20, Jer. 1:19, Gal. 3:13,14, Col. 2:14,15, Matt. 8:17, Mal. 4:2.

PRAYER POINTS

1. You foreign hand laid on my . . ., release me in Jesus' name.
2. In the name of Jesus, I renounce, break and loose myself from all (i) demonic holds (ii) psychic powers (iii) bonds of physical illness and (iv) bondage in Jesus' name.
3. In the name of Jesus, I break and loose myself from all evil curses, chains, spells, jinxes, bewitchments, witchcraft or sorcery which may have been put upon me.
4. Let a creative miracle take place in my . . . organs in Jesus' name.
5. Father, I ask You in the name of Jesus Christ to send out Your angels and have them unearth and break all evil storage vessels fashioned against me.
6. I loose myself from every evil influence, dark spirit and satanic bondage in Jesus' name.
7. I confess and declare that my body is the temple of the Holy Spirit, redeemed, cleansed, and sanctified by the Blood of Jesus Christ.

At the beautiful garden of prayer, waits the Saviour for you.

8. I bind, plunder and render to naught every strongman assigned to my . . . and marital life in Jesus' name.
9. God who quickens the dead should quicken my . . . organs in Jesus' name.
10. I release myself from the hold of spirits of sterility, infertility and fear in Jesus' name.
11. All spirits rooted in fornication, sexual perversion, spirit wives/ husbands, masturbation, guilt, pornography, come out of my . . . organs in Jesus' name.
12. Thank the Lord for your healing and deliverance.

Go with your burden and care to the beautfiul garden of prayer.

PRAYERS FOR COUPLES EXPECTING PROMISED CHILDREN FROM THE LORD

To be done every morning and night.

Scriptures for confession: Psalms 148 - 150, Genesis 1:28, Exodus 23:26, Deut. 7:14, Psalm 127:1-3; 128:3; 113:9, I Timothy 2:15, Galatians 6:17; 3:13,14, Phil. 1:6, Isa. 8:18; 40:5, Exodus 1:19.

Confession:

The Word of God tells me that I should be fruitful and multiply. God said it and I believe it. This must come to pass in my life in Jesus' name. My Father and my God, I bring Your word to remembrance, for You said: "No woman shall be barren in the generation of Abraham". I belong to Christ and I am, therefore, Abraham's seed and heirs according to the promise (Gal. 3:29). Barrenness is a curse of the law and Christ has redeemed me from the curse of the law. I must have my own child by this time next year. You devil, hear the Word of the Lord, all your weapons against me will not prosper in Jesus' name, for the Lord of hosts is with me and the God of Jacob is my refuge. You devil, loose your hold upon my life in Jesus' name, for I bear on my body the mark of Christ. Right now, I command every hindrance to conception, disturbances, blockages in the womb and inherited spirits to depart in Jesus' name. For it is written, "He suffered no man to do them wrong, yea, He reproved kings for their sakes, saying, 'touch not my anointed and do my prophets no harm'". So, you powers of darkness, I am untouchable

---

Just bow and receive a new blessing at the beautiful garden of prayer.

in Jesus' name. The way of fruitfulness has opened for me today. Glory be to the name of the Lord. Amen.

PRAYER POINTS

1. I renounce, denounce and reject every unprofitable covenant regarding childbearing in Jesus' name.
2. I apply the Blood of Jesus Christ to my womb.
3. I bind every hindering spirit in the name of our Lord Jesus Christ.
4. Father in the name of Jesus, work the necessary miracles to enable me have the fruit of the womb.
5. I break every curse of barrenness in the name of Jesus.
6. Lay Your hands upon our lives in the name of Jesus.
7. I command all contrary handwriting against me to be destroyed in Jesus' name.
8. I bind, plunder and render to naught every spirit of infertility and fear in Jesus' name.
9. I loose myself from any curse issued against me by satanic agents in Jesus' name.
10. I release myself from any inherited problem in Jesus' name.
11. I cancel every bewitchment against my reproductive organs and childbearing in Jesus' name.
12. Father Lord, send Your angels to retrieve my blessings from any hiding place in Jesus' name.
13. I renounce and denounce all unprofitable covenants in Jesus' name.
14. Let this month be my month of miracles in Jesus' name.
15. I release myself from every bondage of infertility and pregnancy wastage in Jesus' name.
16. I bind, plunder and render to naught every sperm-destroying and foetal-eating demon in Jesus' name.

Now let us have a little talk with Jesus.

17. I paralyse every spirit behind impotency, ejaculation problems, ovulation failure, hormonal problems and other anti-pregnancy strategies.
18. Lord Jesus, wash away the effect of past sexual sins on my life in Jesus' name.
19. Lord, remove the effect of sexual relationships with demonized partners from my life in Jesus' name.
20. I cancel the evil effects of contaminated menstrual pads and lost underwear in Jesus' name.
21. With the Blood of Jesus, I break every bondage and all ungodly soul ties with all sex partners of the past.

PRAYERS AND CONFESSION AND VICTORY DURING PREGNANCY AND AT CHILD-BIRTH

I declare according to the word of God that the Lord shall perfect everything concerning me. The Lord who has started His good work of creation in me will complete it (Phil. 1:6).

By the power in the blood of the Lord Jesus Christ, I confess that my pregnancy is perfect in the name of Jesus. Every part of my body shall function perfectly for the formation of the baby in Jesus' name. My blood shall circulate effectively. Everything that passes from me to the baby shall be perfect in Jesus' name for the development of the baby. I confess I am strong. Weakness is not my lot in the name of Jesus. I will not have morning sickness or vomiting in my pregnancy in the name of Jesus. I reject cramps, varicose veins, piles and backaches because Jesus Christ has borne all my sicknesses. I refuse constipation, anaemia, vitamin and mineral deficiencies, swollen hands and feet, hypertension, convulsion and diabetes in the mighty name of Jesus. My urine will remain normal in the name of Jesus (Psalm 103: 3-5). I confess that the activities of eaters of flesh and drinkers of blood will not prosper in my life in the name of Jesus. I refuse and reject all negative dreams, visions, prophecies and imaginations in the name of Jesus.

I confess God's Word in Exodus 23:26, that I shall not have a miscarriage, any form of abnormal bleeding or malformation of the baby in Jesus' name. I shall be a joyous mother of children. My womb is fruitful. I am a fruitful vine by the sides of our house. My children are like olive plants round about our table. As the baby

---

He will hear your faintest cry.

grows, every aspect of its growth, formation and development shall be perfect in Jesus' name.

I also confess that I shall not suffer any sickness like nausea, irritation, headache, internal or external pain because by the stripes of Jesus, I am healed. I tread on sickness and upon all the power of the devil. My body is the temple of the Holy spirit. I have the life and health of Christ in me. The Sun of Righteousness has arisen, having conquered sickness and pains, and satan. There is healing in His wings for me. God's will for me and my baby is to prosper and be in good health. God is at work in me now to will and to do His good pleasure. The power of the Holy Spirit is at work in me right now. It is flowing in me and perfecting all that pertains to my baby's formation in Jesus' name.

I declare that every disease and germ should die now in Jesus' name. Nothing I take into my body through the mouth shall harm me nor my baby in Jesus' name. God's Word says, if I drink any deadly thing, it shall not harm me. I confess that as I go to deliver my baby, that the Lord shall direct those taking the delivery what care suits me and the baby in Jesus' name.

My pregnancy is established in righteousness. I am far from oppression. Therefore, I shall not fear, and from terror, because it shall not come near me. No evil shall befall me nor befall my baby, and no plague shall come near my dwelling place and my family.

As the pregnancy progresses, the Lord shall fulfil the number of my days. I shall not have a premature baby but a fully grown baby. My baby shall come out alive, strong and healthy, because nothing shall harm my young. I am fearfully and wonderfully made. My pelvis is wide enough to allow my baby to pass through in the name of Jesus.

I also confess, according to Isaiah 43, that when I pass through the water, the Lord will be with me, if through the rivers, it shall not overflow me and if I walk through the fire, I shall not be burnt nor shall the flame scorch me. Therefore, I confess that I shall pass through the child-delivering without any pain nor hurt in Jesus' name.

The Lord shall take away from me every sickness of pregnancy and child bearing and those that accompany complication according to Deut. 7:14,15. Therefore, I shall not fear because I have been redeemed from the curse of the law - the curse of bringing forth in agony (Galatians 4).

I boldly confess Isaiah 66:7 that before I travail, I will give birth and before any pain comes, I will be delivered of my baby. Moreover, according to 1 Tim. 2:15, I will be delivered of my baby. Moreover, according to 1 Tim. 2:15, I will be saved in child bearing because I continue in faith, love and holiness with self-control.

I confess I shall go to the delivery room confidently in Jesus' name. The Lord has given me perfect peace because my mind rests on Him. My trust is in the Lord and Jehovah God is my everlasting strength.

According to Psalm 118:17, I confess that I shall not die at childbirth, nor shall my baby suffer death. We shall both live to declare the works of the Lord in Jesus' name. My cervix shall be fully dilated and the passage big and open enough to allow the baby pass through with ease. The delivery shall be perfect in Jesus' name. No evil shall befall me nor my baby. No weapon of the devil that is fashioned against me nor against my baby shall prosper in Jesus' name.

The Lord is the strength of my life, of whom shall I be afraid. He is my Deliverer, my God, my Buckler and the Horn of my Salvation. The Lord is all I need to take through on that day. He will strengthen the bars of my gate. He has blessed my children within me. Therefore, through the Lord I shall do valiantly. I will live to be the happy mother of my baby. None of us shall see death in Jesus' name. I refuse prolonged labour and reject all pains from the devil during labour and afterwards.

I look forward to the rearing of the children after birth. I confess we shall bring them up in the way of the Lord. The children shall grow up to know and love the Lord from their youth. I also confess that the Lord shall supply all our needs during pregnancy and for the

---

babies after their delivery in Jesus' name.
Glory be to the name of the Lord, because I shall have what I say in Jesus' name.

PRAYER POINTS

Stand against the following things aggressively in the mighty name of Jesus every morning and night.

1. Early morning sickness
2. Miscarriages
3. Swollen hands and feet
4. Abnormal vaginal bleeding and anaemia
5. Backache, cramps, varicose veins
6. Convulsion in pregnancy
7. Hypertension and Diabetes Mellitus
8. Complicated and aided child delivery, e.g. operations or instruments
9. Unnatural tiredness or weakness during pregnancy
10. Demonic Midwives and Doctors
11. Requirement of blood transfusion
12. Premature delivery and late delivery
13. Anti-pregnancy satanic dreams
14. Spirit of fear and still-birth
15. Satanic dreams of blood and the activities of pregnancy-sucking spirits
16. Demonic exchange of the baby in the womb and
17. Evil observers, satanic diary and wicked date calculators.

Be violent spiritually. Pray in your spirit language and be aggressive. Try and do occasional short night vigils. Form the habit of laying your hands on the pregnancy and prophesy good things on your baby.

You must fight and be brave against all evil - keep on the firring line.

VIOLENT PRAYERS AGAINST STUBBORN PROBLEMS AND FOUNDATIONAL ENEMIES

Confession: Psalm 2:9, Obad. 1:3,4, Deut. 33:27 Isa. 49:25,26, Psalms 109; 17:29; 76:6; 129:5,6

PRAYER POINTS

1. Lord, unveil the innermost secrets behind this problem to me in the mighty name of Jesus.
2. Lord, reveal unto me the areas that need aggressive prayer action in my life in Jesus' name.
3. Lord, send Your Elisha to my Jericho-like situation in the name of Jesus.
4. Lord, speak the words of ressurection, power and deliverance to every organ of my body *(lay your hand on any problematic part of your body)* in the name of Jesus.
5. Let all the affairs of my life be withdrawn from evil records in the name of Jesus.
6. Let all the enemies in the camp of my life be disarmed in the mighty name of Jesus.
7. Let all stubborn enemies of my well-being eat their own flesh and drink their own blood in the name of Jesus.
   (Sing the chorus: "Let God arise and His enemies be scattered).
8. Let all evil names affecting me negatively be changed by the Holy Spirit in the name of Jesus.

Take your burden to the Lord and leave it there.

9. All curses, evil covenants and evil decisions holding down my miracle should be revoked in the name of Jesus.
10. I dissociate myself from any unconscious evil vow, oath, agreement and covenants in the name of Jesus.
11. Let all the executors of demonic decisions against my life be cast into a dead sleep in the mighty name of Jesus.
12. Let every evil thing working against me in the second heavens, on earth, in any body or water and underneath the earth be pulled down and smashed in the name of Jesus.
13. Let me receive miraculous divine visitations that will end the problem in the name of Jesus.
14. All strange friends, strange fires and strange organizations arranged for my downfall will not prosper in Jesus' name.
15. I curse the spirit of spiritual and marital barrenness in the name of Jesus.
16. I loose myself from any bondage that I have entered into through bad friends and parents.

BREAKING STUBBORN YOKES AND EVIL COVENANTS

73

Praise Worship: Songs of Worship
Confession: Col. 2:14 Gal. 3:13,14, Psalms 71:21; 56:9; 138:8, Rom. 16:20, Zech. 4:7-9

PRAYER POINTS

1. I forgive all who have hurt or disappointed me in Jesus' name.
2. Lord, forgive me and I also forgive myself for all my many faults and failures in Jesus' name.
3. I break every power and covenant associated with any incision on my body and I release myself from their grip in Jesus' name.
4. I renounce and denounce any conscious or unconscious association with familiar spirits and spirit husbands.
5. In the name of Jesus Christ, I now renounce, break and loose myself from all demonic subjection or control and from any ungodly soul-tie.
6. I break any curse that is negatively affecting my spiritual or physical life which may be in my family even back to ten generations on both sides of the family in Jesus' name.
7. Let every evil mark be rubbed off in the name of Jesus.
8. I cancel every negative prophesy issued against my life in Jesus' name.

Are you weary, are you heavey hearted? Tell it to Jesus.

9. The Lord should reveal to me every secret about my life in Jesus' name.

10. I renounce and break myself loose from all evil curses, charms, jinxes, spells, hexes, pshycic powers, bewitchments, witchcraft or sorcery which may have been put upon me or my family in Jesus' name.

11. I renounce all the spirits connected and related to the above and command them to leave me now.

12. I withdraw all the materials belonging to me from every evil altar in Jesus' name.

13. I release myself from the influence and activities of water spirits and fake prophets.

14. Father in the name of Jesus, send Your angels to unearth and break all demonic storage vessels and pictures buried on my behalf.

15. I confess that my body is the temple of the Holy Spirit, redeemed, cleansed and sanctified by the Blood of Jesus. Therefore, satan has no more place in me, no power over me because of Jesus.

16. Let the earth swallow my Korah, Dathan and Abiram in the name of Jesus.

17. Let every evil river flowing into my life dry up in the name of Jesus.

18. Let every thought of evil against me be turned to good in Jesus' name.

19. Lord, expose all hidden evil friends in Jesus' name.

20. I refuse to enter into the net of evil constructed by the enemies of my soul in Jesus' name.

21. Let every evil spirit guard be rendered impotent in the name of Jesus.

22. No matter what rulers are in charge, let my blessings, goodness and prosperity pursue me in the name of Jesus.

Are you grieving over joys departed? Tell it to Jesus.

23. I refuse to tarry in satanic bus stop in the name of Jesus.
24. I decree that my environment should work to my favour in Jesus' name.
25. O Lord, keep my spirit safe from spiritual accident.
26. I refuse to be used as an evil example in the mighty name of Jesus.
27. Let the spirit of laziness and amputation depart from my life in Jesus' name.
28. I bind every spirit of lukewarmness in the mighty name of Jesus.
29. O Lord, revive my spiritual life from the hands of the oppressors.

RELEASE
FROM THE
EVIL EFFECTS
OF POLYGAMY

Confession: Col. 1:13-15, Num. 23:23, Rom. 16:20, Deut. 28:4; 7:15

PRAYER POINTS

1. Every problem linked to polygamy that is affecting my life negatively should be dissolved by the fire of the Holy Ghost.
2. Every evil done against my life by my fathers' wives or concubines should be nullified in Jesus' name.
3. I break every curse of marriage destruction.
4. Every problem linked to my head and my body system should be removed in Jesus' name.
5. Every spirit that entered in through herbal concoction should depart from my life in Jesus' name.
6. Every night and dream attacks and its consequences should be nullified in Jesus' name.
7. Every spirit associated with consultation of herbalists should depart from me now in Jesus' name.
8. I cancel any demonic name and the associated transfer of evil things in Jesus' name.
9. Every spirit linked to Idol-worship should depart from my life in Jesus' name.

Do you fear the gathering clouds of sorrow? Tell it to Jesus.

10. I cancel evil effects of demonic solutions to my problems in Jesus' name.
11. Lay your hands on the lower abdomen and ask God for a creative miracle.
12. Let every evil thing introduced into my life by any demonic relationship be removed in Jesus' name.
13. I cancel any demonic marriage and child bearing in Jesus' name.
14. I break every curse of sterility, infertility and loneliness.

UPROOTING THE PROBLEMS USING THE BATTLE AXE

PRAYER POINTS

1. Curses of impossiblity, I nullify you in Jesus' name.
2. I break down every high evil stronghold in my life built by my own mouth in Jesus' name.
3. Father Lord, give me a divine prescription for all my problems in Jesus' name.
4. Lord, send Your axe of fire to the root of all problems that I have and cut them down in Jesus' name.
5. I refuse to be a candidate of selective misfortune in the name of Jesus.
6. You spirit of Jezebel, you will not kill the prophet within me in Jesus' name.
7. O Lord, restore back unto me every thing that I have lost through my stepping into the net of the fowler.
8. Father Lord, help me to re-arrange my priority to be Your own priority.
9. O Lord, send Your fire to dissolve any deeply rooted problem I might have.
10. I refuse to enter into the valley of failure designed for me through inheritance.
11. Lord Jesus, wash away any repercussion of any unclean money spent on me by my parent.

For Christ's coming, daily are you sighing? Tell it to Jesus.

12. O Lord, heal me from any spiritual injury.

13. I refuse to be a spiritual basket, I will retain my miracle.

14. I bind every spirit of disunity in my home in Jesus' name.

15. Lord, carry out any necessary surgical operation in my life.

16. Let the fire of the Holy Ghost quench every arrow of prayerlessness fired at me the by enemies of my soul in Jesus' name.

17. I claim myself back from the grip of any spirit that has altered me contrary to Holy Ghost in Jesus' name.

18. I command every evil load and their vessel of transportation, to fall after the order of Senacherib in Jesus' name.

19. O Lord, reveal to me who I am.

20. O Lord, I repent from anything that I've done to aid my enemy.

21. Let any organ in my body that any strange hand is laid upon, be released in Jesus' name.

22. Let any of my blessing currently in bondage in the body of a river, be released in Jesus' name.

23. All imported problems in my life should go back to the senders in Jesus' name.

24. Lord, help me to do the right thing at the right time in Jesus' name.

25. Let every spirit of Pharaoh refusing to let me go and serve my God, die in Jesus' name.

26. I break the head of every serpentine spirit working against my life in Jesus' name.

27. I reject the use of my life as a demonic game in Jesus' name.

28. All devices of the enemy slowing down my progress spiritually and physically, be destroyed in Jesus' name.

29. Let all physical and spiritual powers sitting on my promotion be unseated in Jesus' name.

30. I withdraw my virtue from the hands of evil possessors.

For Christ's coming, daily are you sighing? Tell it to Jesus.

31. Let all fountain of inherited evil dry up in Jesus' name.
32. Father Lord, erase paralysing ease from every area of my life.
33. Let all trees of non-achievement whether physical or spiritual, be uprooted in Jesus' name.
34. O God, let Your fire destroy any foundational problem that I have.
35. Father Lord, crucify everything within me that will remove my name from the book of life.
36. Let all satanic reinforcements against me, be scattered in Jesus' name.
37. Let any clock or time table of the enemy for my life, be roasted.
38. Let every dead organ of my body receive life in Jesus' name.
39. Let Your kingdom be established in every area of my life.
40. Let any power gluing me to any problem, be roasted in the name of Jesus.
41. I release myself from any remote control power contrary to the will of God in the name of Jesus.
42. Let every yoke of the enemy present in my life/home, be destroyed in the name of Jesus.
43. I command every evil spiritual record bearing my name to be roasted in Jesus' name.
44. Let all hindrances to the manifestation of the Holy Spirit, depart from my life in Jesus' name.
45. All foreign hands covering my blessing, be roasted in Jesus' name.
46. You satanic power, vomit all my blessings that you have swallowed in Jesus' name.
47. Lord, forgive me for not opening enough room for the Holy Spirit.
48. Let the Rock of Ages smash into pieces all hindrances to my breakthrough.

49. Let every attack of my enemy be converted to promotion after the order of Shadrach, Mesach and Abdnego.
50. Let the evil worms eating away the roots of any good thing in my life be roasted in the name of Jesus.

It is very sweet to trust in Jesus in prayer.

IGNITING THE FIRE OF THE HOLY GHOST

Memory Verse: Isaiah 64:1

Hymn: **COME HOLY SPIRIT**

The Ho-ly Spir-it came at Pen-te-cost,
He came in might-y full-ness then;
His wit-ness thru be-liev-ers won the lost
And mul-ti-tudes were born a-gain
The ear-ly Chris-tians scattered o'er the world
They preached the gospel fear-less-ly;
Tho some were mar-tyred and to li-ons hurled,
They marched a-long in vic-to-ry!
    Come, Ho-ly Spir-it, Dark is the hour,
    We need Your fill-ing, You love and Your might-y pow'r;
    Move now a-mong us, Stir us, we pray,
    Come, Ho-ly Spir-it, Re-vive the Church to-day.
Then in an age when dark-nes gripped the earth,
"The just shall live by faith" was learned;
The Ho-ly Spir-it gave the Church new birth,
As ref-or-mation fire burned
In lat-er years the great re-viv-als came,
When saints would seek the Lord and pray;
O once a-gain we need that ho-ly flame
To meet the chal-lenge of to-day.

It is very sweet to trust in Jesus in prayer.

PRAYER POINTS

1. Thank the Lord for the Holy Spirit.
2. Confession of sins and repentance.
3. Let the Holy Spirit fill me afresh.
4. Let every unbroken area in my life be broken in Jesus' name.
5. Father, incubate me with fire of the Holy Spirit.
6. Let every anti-power bondage break in my life in Jesus' name.
7. Let all strangers flee away from my spirit and let the Holy Spirit take control.
8. Lord, catapult my spiritual life to the mountain top.
9. Lord, fill me with spiritual gifts.
10. Let heavens open and let the glory of God fall upon me.
11. Let signs and wonders be my lot in Jesus' name.
12. Let the joy of the oppressors about my life be turned into sorrow.
13. Let all multiple strongman operating against me be paralysed in Jesus' name.
14. Lord, open my eyes and ears to receive wondrous things from You.
15. Lord, grant me victory over every temptation and satanic device.
16. Lord, ignite my spiritual life so that I will stop fishing in unprofitable waters.
17. Lord, release the Pentecostal tongue of fire to burn away all spiritual filthiness in my life.
18. Father, make me to hunger and thirst for righteousness in Jesus' name.
19. Lord, help me to be ready to do the Lord's work without expecting any recognition from others.
20. Lord, give me victory over emphasizing the weaknesses and sins of other people while ignoring my own.
21. O Lord, give me depth and rootage in my faith.

Tell Jesus of your trials.

22. O Lord, heal every dot of backsliding in my spiritual life.
23. Lord, help me to be willing to serve others rather than wanting to exercise authority.
24. Lord, open my understanding concerning scriptures.
25. Lord, help me to live each day recognizing that the day will come when You will judge secret lives and innermost thoughts.
26. Lord, let me be willing to be the clay in Your hands ready to be molded as You desire.
27. Lord, wake me up out of any form of spiritual sleep and help me to put on the armour of light.
28. Lord, give me victory over all carnality and help me to be in the center of Your will.
29. I stand against anything in my life that will cause others to stumble in Jesus' name.
30. Lord, enable me to run the Christian race with certainty and not be one who is just beating the air.
31. Lord, help me to put away childish things and put on maturity.
32. I stand against all forms of darkened understanding, blinded and hardened heart in Jesus' name.
33. Lord, empower me to stand firm against all the schemes and techniques of the devil.
34. O Lord, help me to fight the good fight of faith.
35. Lord, let me get on fire for You.
36. Lord, give me a big appetite for the pure milk and solid food in the Word.
37. Lord, empower me to stay away from anything or anybody that might take God's place in my heart.

PRAYING THE AGGRESSIVE PRAYERS OF THE PSALMIST

The Psalmist understood spiritual warfare. His prayer points may appear to be too hot for junior students in the school of spiritual warfare, because it contains dreadful pronouncements against the enemies of God.

The Psalms is a handbook on the warfare of the righteous against demon forces.

Many Christians claim that the prayers of the Psalmist contradicts our Lord's injunction to love your enemies. It is a sin to hate any human being. It is also a sin to love demons. The Psalmist refused to kill King Saul, his human enemy, even when confronted with the opportunity.

You must pray against spiritual enemies and not human foes who are mere instruments. Always remember, the only language understood by the enemies of our soul is VIOLENCE and RESOUNDING DEFEAT. Spiritual warfare prayers are to be directed against the powers of darkness rather than towards a person.

Use the prayer points of the Psalmist when things look stubborn; unyielding and defiant.

PRAYER POINTS

1. Let the powers of the wicked be blown away as the chaff which the wind is driving away in the name of Jesus.

In your distress, He kindly will help you.

2. Let the way of the wicked powers assigned to any department in my life perish in Jesus' name.
3. The Lord should laugh to scorn all evil counsellors against me.
4. The Lord should have the evil kings gathered for my sake in derision.
5. The Lord should break them with a rod of iron.
6. The Lord should dash them in pieces like a potter's vessel.
7. The Lord should smite all my enemies upon the cheek bone.
8. The Lord should break the teeth of the wicked.
9. O Lord, destroy the enemies using poisonous tongues and sepulchre throat against my life.
10. Let the enemies fall by their own counsels in Jesus' name.
11. Let wicked be casted out in the multitude of their transgression in Jesus' name.
12. O Lord, let all my enemies be ashamed and be sore vexed.
13. O Lord, let all my enemies receive sudden shame and return their arrows.
14. Arise, O Lord in Your anger and lift up Yourself because of the rage of my enemies.
15. O Lord, let the wickedness of the wicked come to an end.
16. O Lord, prepare the instruments of death against my persecutors.
17. O Lord, ordain Your arrows against my persecutors.
18. O Lord, let the enemies of my soul fall into the pit which they made.
19. O Lord, let the mischief of the oppressors return upon their own heads.
20. O Lord, let the violent dealing of the enemy come down upon his own path.
21. Lord, let my enemies fall and perish at Your presence.

Tell Jesus of your troubles, He is a kind, compassionate friend.

22. Lord, let the net of the enemy take up his own feet.
23. Let the wicked be taken in devices that they have imagined.
24. Lord, break the arm of the wicked.
25. Let the sorrows of my enemies be multiplied.
26. Arise Lord, disappoint the enemy and deliver my soul from the wicked.
27. Let the thunder, hailstones, coals of fire, lightening and arrows from the Lord scatter the forces of the enemy.
28. Lord, give unto me the necks of mine enemies.
29. Let all oppressors be beaten small as the dust before the wind.
30. Let them be casted out as the dirt in the streets.
31. The Lord should swallow the oppressors and persecutors in His wrath.
32. Lord, let the fire devour the wicked and their seeds.
33. Lord, deliver my soul from the power of the dog and from the mouth of the lion.
34. Lord, let all the mischevious devices of the enemy refuse to perform.
35. Let all the eater of flesh and drinkers of blood stumble and fall in the name of Jesus.
36. Lord, render to my enemies their desert.
37. Let all lips speaking grievous things proudly and contemptuously against me be silenced in Jesus' name.
38. Lord, send Your angels to sow terror and panic in the hearts of all witch-doctors gathered for my sake.
39. Evil shall slay the wicked and they that hate the righteous shall be desolate.
40. O Lord, fight against them that fight against me.
41. Let them be confounded and put to shame that seek after my soul.

Jesus will all your cares and sorrows share.

42. Let them be turned back and brought to confusion that devise my hurt.
43. Let the angels of the Lord chase and persecute the enemies of my soul.
44. Let the way of my enemies be darkened and slippery.
45. Let destruction come upon my enemies unawares.
46. Lord, let not them that are mine enemies wrongfully rejoice over me neither let them wink the eye that hate me without a cause.
47. Let them be ashamed and brought to confusion together that rejoice at my hurt.
48. Let them be clothed with shame and dishonour that magnify themselves against me.
49. Let the sword of the wicked enter into their own heart and let their bows be broken.
50. All the enemies of the Lord shall be as the fat of lambs, in smoke shall they consume away.
51. Let all my enemies be laid in the grave like a sheep and let death feed on them.
52. O Lord, destroy and divide the tongues of the enemy.
53. O God, break the teeth of the enemy in their mouth.
54. Let them melt away as waters which run continually.
55. When the enemy bends his bows to shoot his arrows, let them be cut in pieces.
56. Let every one of the oppressors pass away like the untimely birth of a woman that they may not see the sun.
57. Let them wander up and down for meat and grudge if they be not satisfied.
58. Let the wicked fall by the sword and become a portion for foxes.
59. God shall wound the head of the enemy and the hairy scalp of the wicked.

60. Let their table become a snare before them.
61. Let that which should have been for their welfare become a trap.
62. Let the extortioner catch all that the enemy has, and let the strangers spoil his labour.
63. As he loved cursing, so let it come unto him; as he delighted not in blessing, so let it be far from him.
64. Let them be as grass upon the house tops which withers before it grows up.
65. Lord, stretch forth Your hand against my enemies.
66. Let the mischief of their own lips cover them.
67. Grant not O Lord, the desires of the wicked, further not his wicked device.
68. Let burning coals fall upon them.
69. Let them be cut into fire and the deep pit that they rise not up again.
70. Let their eyes be darkened that they see not.
71. Make their loins shake continuously.
72. Let their habitations become desolate, let there be no one to dwell in them.
73. Add iniquity unto their iniquity.
74. Let them be covered with reproach and dishonour that seek my hurt.
75. Persecute them with tempest and make them afraid with Thy storm.
76. Mine eyes also shall see my desire on my enemies and mine ears shall hear my desire of the wicked that rise up against me.
77. Let his children be continually vagabonds and become beggars, let them seek their bread out of desolate places.
78. Let evil hunt the violent enemy to overthrown him.

Blessed hour of prayer - what a balm for the weary.

79. O Lord, cast forth lightening and scatter them.
80. Let God arise and let all His enemies be scattered.

78 HEALING THE WOUNDED SPIRIT

Confession: Isa. 53:5, Rom. 12:2, John 14:27, Luke 10:27, Phil. 4:7, Col. 1:13, 2 Cor. 3:11, Heb. 13:8, Phil. 3:13, Heb. 4:12, Psalm 18:2, Luke 10:19, Psalm 51:10, 1 Thessa. 5:23

PRAYER POINTS

1. I forgive all those who offended me and I also forgive myself in Jesus' name.
2. Lord Jesus, walk through every second of my life to heal me and make me whole.
3. Lord, go back into the 3rd and 4th generations and break all unprofitable family ties.
4. Lord, set me free from any negative force transmitted to me in my mother's womb.
5. Lord use Your spiritual eraser to wipe off all painful memories of the past.
6. Lord, repair any damage done to my spirit by satanic agents.
7. I command every covenant of failure to break in the name of Jesus.
8. Lord, awaken any area of my spirit still sleeping.
9. I cancel all death wishes in the name of Jesus.
10. Pray for divine healing for any spiritual disease.

Give me more power in prayer, Lord Jesus.

11. I release myself from all uptightness, fear, jumpiness and guilt feelings in Jesus' name.
12. I release myself from every form of anger, bitter root expectation, deep sadness and depression in the name of Jesus.
13. I release myself from every rejection caused by the manner of birth in the name of Jesus.
14. I release myself from any rejection caused by the manner of timing of conception in the name of Jesus.
15. I release myself from any problem that has come to me through:
    - (a) being born with the sex opposite to what the parent desired
    - (b) subjection to sexual molestation or perversion
    - (c) being called degrading names
    - (d) parental cruelty
    - (e) broken homes
    - (f) broken engagement or rejection in love
    - (g) failure to be forgiven or trusted by parent.

There shall be showers of blessings.

FREEDOM FROM CAGED LIFE

PRAYER POINTS

1. Let all evil spiritual padlocks be roasted by the fire of God in the name of Jesus.
2. Let all buried goodness and prosperity be released in the name of Jesus.
3. I break and loose myself from the curse and ordination of untimely death in the name of Jesus.
4. Let the evil effects of obtaining children, wife and husband from the wrong sources be nullified in the name of Jesus.
5. Let all the problems associated with physical or spiritual poison be nullified in the name of Jesus.
6. Let all the problems associated with bad inheritance and names break in the name of Jesus.
7. Let all evil cages trapping my goodness and potentials be roasted in Jesus' name.

From every stormy wind that blows, From every swelling tide of woes.

PRAYERS FOR SALVATION OF RELATIVES OR FRIENDS

Confession: Eph. 1:16-23; 3:14-21, Psalms 21:2; 86:16, Isa. 49:25; 54:13; 2:6; 49:25, Hosea 2:6-15

PRAYER POINTS

1. Father in the name of Jesus, give unto . . . *(mention the name of the person)*, the spirits of wisdom and revelation in the knowledge of You.

2. Let every stronghold of the enemy barricading the mind of . . . *(mention the name of the person)*, from receiving the Lord be pulled down in the name of Jesus.

3. Let all hindrances coming between the heart of . . . *(mention the name of the person)* and the gospel be melted away by the Fire of the Holy Spirit.

4. I bind the strongman attached to the life of . . . *(mention the name of the person)*, from keeping him from receiving Jesus Christ as his Lord and Saviour in the name of Jesus.

5. The Lord should build a hedge of thorns around . . . *(mention the name of the person)*, so that he turns to the Lord.

6. All the children who have been dedicated to the Lord and then became bound, should be loosed in the name of Jesus.

7. In the name of Jesus, I break the curse placed on . . . *(mention the name of the person)*, binding him from receiving the Lord.

There is a calm, a sure retreat - 'Tis found beneath the mercy seat.

8. You spirit of death and hell, release . . . *(mention the name of the person)* in the name of Jesus.

9. Every desire of the enemy on the soul of . . . *(mention the name of the person)*, will not prosper in the name of Jesus.

10. You spirit of destruction, release . . . *(mention the name of the person)* in the name of Jesus.

11. I bind every spirit of mind blindness in the life of . . . *(mention the name of the person)* in the name of Jesus.

12. Let there be no peace or rest in the mind of . . . *(mention the name of the person)* until he surrenders to the Lord Jesus Christ.

13. Spirit of bondage, lukewarmness and perdition, release . . . *(mention the name of the person)* in the name of Jesus.

14. Lord, open the eyes of . . . *(mention the name of the person)* to his own spiritual condition in the name of Jesus.

There is a place where Jesus sheds The oil of gladness on our heads.

PRAYERS FOR THOSE DESIRING SOUND SLEEP

Sleeplessness or insomnia is not from the Lord. These prayers should be done aggressively. If you had a bad night, you're likely to have a bad day.

Confession: Psalms 3:5; 4:8; 127:2, Prov. 3:24, Eccl. 5:12, Isa. 29:10, Luke 9:32, Psalm 121

Lord Jesus, I thank You for Your day time and for Your night time. I know You never sleep but constantly watch over me. I know You have placed Your guardian angels all around me.

Lord, I give You all my cares and my worries of the day. I give You all my fears.

Satan, I bind you from me in the name of Jesus. All spirits of fear, especially fear of the dark, you are bound from me in the name of Jesus. I rebuke the fear of fire and fear of intruders in the name of Jesus. Spirits of insomnia, nervousness, tension, worry, I cast you out in the name of Jesus.

Lord, please go into the darkest recesses of my mind, into my subconscious, into the dream area, and heal all painful memories and trauma.

Lord, I ask You to fill me with Your divine love, Your peace, Your calmness. I pray You will allow me to sleep soundly all night long and wake up feeling refreshed in the morning. I commit myself to You.

It's in the name of Jesus that I pray. Amen.

A place than all besides more sweet - It is the blood-bought mercy seat.

PRAYER POINTS

1. Thank you Father for the protection offered under Your unsleeping eye in the name of Jesus.
2. I commend my body, soul and spirit to Your care O Father as I sleep in Jesus' name.
3. Father, in the name of Jesus, let me not go through any part of this night unaccompanied by Thee.
4. I claim sound sleep and refreshing sleep in the name of Jesus.
5. I claim safety from all perils of the night in Jesus' name.
6. I claim protection from the arrows of destruction and pestilences of the night in Jesus' name.
7. I claim freedom from satanic and restless dreams in Jesus' name.
8. I claim freedom from importing anxiety and shameful thoughts into my dream in Jesus' name.
9. Father, let me experience the brightness of Thy presence.
10. Intercede in the spirit for all those who cannot sleep for pain or for anxiety.
11. Thank the Lord for His redemptive power and the power of the Cross to deliver from the chains of the enemy.
12. I release myself from the bondage of sleeplessness in the name of Jesus.
13. I break the yoke of the oppressors in the name of Jesus.
14. I bind every spirit of fear or infirmity preventing me from enjoying sound sleep in the name of Jesus.
15. I release myself from the bondage of early unprofitable waking up in the name of Jesus.
16. Let every emotional strain, nightmare, anxiety or depression initiating sleeplessness be melted away by the fire of the Holy Spirit in the name of Jesus.

There is a place of quiet rest, Near to the heart of God.

17. I receive deliverance from bondage of sleeping tablets in the name of Jesus.
18. I claim sound and sweet sleep in the mighty name of Jesus.
19. Let every sleep disturbance originator be eliminated from my life in the name of Jesus.
20. I bind every spirit of faintness, dizziness, headache, tremour, unusual sweating, poor concentration, palpitation diarrhoea and any other spirit causing difficulty in sleeping in Jesus' name.
21. Every sleeplessness attached to previous horrifying experiences should be dismantled.
22. The fear of going to sleep should be eliminated from every area of my life in the name of Jesus.
23. Let the name of the Lord be glorified in every area of my life.

82 DELIVERANCE FROM MENTAL ILLNESS

Praises *(e.g. How great Thou art)*
Song - *There is power mighty in the Blood.*
Confessions

- **Psalm 25:16**: *Turn thee unto me, and have mercy upon me; for I am desolate and afflicted.*
- **Psalm 25:17**: *The troubles of my heart are enlarged: O bring thou me out of my distresses.*
- **Psalm 25:20**: *O keep my soul, and deliver me: let me not be ashamed; for I put my trust in thee.*
- **Psalm 9:9**: *The Lord also will be a refuge for the oppressed, a refuge in times of trouble.*
- **Isa. 50:7**: *For the Lord God will help me; therefore shall I not be confounded: therefore have I set my face like a flint and I know that I shall not be ashamed.*
- **2Cor. 10:5b**: *. . . bringing into captivity every thought to the obedience of Christ.*
- **Phil. 4:7**: *And the peace of God, which passeth all understanding, shall keep you HEARTS and MINDS though Christ Jesus.*
- **2Tim. 1:7**: *For God hath not given us the spirit of fear; but of power, and of love, and of a sound mind.*

There is a place of comfort sweet, Near the heart of God.

PRAYER POINTS

1. Father, I confess that, in the past, I had held unforgiveness, sometime bitterness and resentment in my heart against certain people who had hurt or disappointed me.

2. I now recognise this as a sin and confess it as sin, for You have said in Your Word that if we confess our sin, You are faithful and just to forgive us our sin and to cleanse us of all unrighteousness (1 John 1:9).

3. I do now forgive the following people, whom I can remember, who have hurt or disappointed me. *(Mention names of those who come to your mind.)* I now freely forgive all these people and ask You to bless them if they are living. I also forgive myself for all my many faults and failures, for You have freely forgiven me.

4. Thank You Father for freedom from the load of unforgiveness, bitterness and resentment in Jesus' name.

   Father, I confess to You, that in the past, through ignorance, through curiosity or through wilfulness, I have come into contact with certain sinful acts. I now recognise this as sin and confess it as sin, claiming forgiveness in the name of Jesus.

5. I also renounce and confess as sin any oath which I have made to any false god and any idolatry in which I have been involved.

6. Satan, I rebuke you in the name of Jesus, and I am closing any door which I or my ancestors may have opened to you and your demons in the name of Jesus.

7. I renounce satan and all his demons, I declare them to be my enemies and I command them out of my life completely in the name of Jesus.

8. In the name of Jesus Christ, I now claim deliverance from any and all evil spirits which may be in me (Joel 2:28). Once and for all, I close the door in my life to all occult practices and command all related spirits to leave me now in Jesus' name.

9. I break every curse of mental destruction in the name of Jesus.

A place where we and our Saviour meet, Near the heart of God.

10. I release myself from the hold of any evil strongman in the name of Jesus.

11. I command all spirits of confusion to loose their hold upon my life in the name of Jesus.

12. *Call the spirit you do not desire in your life by name. Then issue the command firmly and repeatedly that the spirits must come out in the name of the Lord Jesus.*

    Pray as follows: You spirit of . . . ,

1. Mental illness	2.	Hallucinations
3. Insanity	4.	Lunacy
5. Neuroses	6.	Anxiety
7. Depression	8.	Hysteria
9. Compulsive behaviours	10.	Personality disorders
11. Sexual deviation	12.	Alcoholism
13. Premature Aging	14.	Double-mindedness
15. Retardation	16.	Convulsion
17. Vandalism	18.	Murder
19. Destruction	20.	Rage
21. Black out	22.	Mind darkness
23. Incoherence	24.	Mind dullness
25. Apathy	26.	Day dreaming
27. Inactivity	28.	Indifference
29. Slowness	30.	Stupidity
31. Trance	32.	Unreasonable behaviours

    33. Addiction for and bondage to drugs of:-

- Marijuana	- LSD (acid)	- Cocaine
- Heroin	- Valium-	- Amphetamines
- Barbiturates	- Tranquilizers	- Aspirin
- Caffeine	- Nicotine	- Any drug

    Come out of my brain and mind in the name of Jesus.

16. I loose myself from you in the name of Jesus, and I command you to leave me right now in the mighty name of our Lord Jesus Christ.

O Jesus, blest Redeemer, sent from the heart of God.

BAPTIJM BY FIRE

Scriptures for meditation: 2 Chronicles 6; 7:1-6
Confession: Jer. 20:9

PRAYER POINTS

1. Thank God for the purifying power of the fire of the Holy Ghost.
2. I cover myself with the blood of the Lord Jesus.
3. Father, let Your fire that burns away every deposit of the enemy fall upon me in the name of Jesus .
4. Holy Ghost fire, incubate me in the name of the Lord Jesus Christ.
5. I reject any evil stamp or seal placed upon me by ancestral spirits in the name of Jesus.
6. I release myself from every negative anointing in the name of Jesus.
7. Let every door of spiritual leakage be closed in the name of Jesus.
8. I challenge every organ of my body with the fire of the Holy Spirit. *(Lay your right hand methodically on various parts of the body beginning from the head.)*
9. Let every human spirit attacking my own spirit release me in the mighty name of Jesus.

Daniel prayed in the morning, afternoon and in the evening - he shook kingdom.

10. I reject every spirit of the tail in the name of Jesus.

11. Sing the song "Holy Ghost fire, fire fall on me".

12. Let all evil marks on my body be burnt off by the fire of the Holy Spirit in the name of Jesus.

13. Let the anointing of the Holy Ghost fall upon me and break every negative yoke in the name of Jesus.

14. Let every garment of hindrance and dirtiness be dissolved by the fire of the Holy Ghost in the name of Jesus.

15. I command all my chained blessings to be unchained in the name of Jesus.

16. Let all spiritual cages inhibiting my progress be roasted by the fire of the Holy Spirit in the name of Jesus.

Now Make this Powerful Confession Before You Proceed

I boldly declare that my body is the temple of God and that the Holy Ghost is dwelling in me.

I am cleansed through the blood of the Lord Jesus Christ. Therefore, whosoever wants me to go into captivity shall go into captivity. Whosoever wants me to die by the sword shall die by the sword. The strangers shall fade away and be afraid out of their close places in the mighty name of the Lord Jesus Christ. They shall lick the dust like a serpent, they shall move out of their holes like worms of the earth, they shall be afraid of the Lord our GOD.

17. I refuse to harbour any strange property in any department of my body in the name of Jesus.

18. I command the evil effect of any strange hand laid upon my life to be nullified in the name of Jesus.

19. I vomit and pass out of my system any satanic deposit in my head, stomach, reproductive organs and legs in the name of Jesus. *(Remain silent after 20 such aggressive commands and breathe in and out several times, then repeat the command as you transfer your hand to a different part of the body.)*

Jacob prayed and fought through with the angel - his life changed.

20. Let every hidden sickness depart now in the name of Jesus.
21. I command any bewitched food consumed by me to receive the fire of God and come out of their hidding places.
22. I release myself from any unconscious bondage in the name of Jesus.
23. Holy Ghost fire, do the work of purification in my life.
24. Lord, I come to You in the name of Jesus as Your Child, reminding You of Your most holy promise to set free all those who call upon Your merciful name. Lord Jesus, set me free now.
25. In the mighty name of Jesus Christ of Nazareth, I come against every spirit and god of air, fire and water, nature and every idol and animal deity in my life.
26. I break their stronghold over me and my blood line back unto the first generation of idolaters, and release myself from the sin of idolatry.
27. I cancel the effects of every evil birth dedication and annul every ungodly covenant set up by Satan over my life in the name of Jesus.
28. I sever myself from every ungodly prediction and every commitment and dedication made for me at birth or by myself later on in the name of Jesus.
29. I loose myself from the bondage of every ungodly covenant and dedication in Jesus' holy name.
30. I cut every soul tie with any serpentine spirit in the name of Jesus.
31. I excise the poison and venom of the scorpions and serpents, the accuser and destroyer from my flesh in Jesus' name.
32. I cut myself off from the curse of evil consumption e.g. drinking of blood, eating meat sacrificed to idols, contaminated meals from demonic parties, of medicine man or witchdoctor portions by myself and my ancestors, and from diagnosis or foretelling

Elijah prayed - and stopped the rain.

by the use of satanic materials or any other ungodly tool in Jesus' mighty name.

33. In Jesus' name, I now pull down the stronghold of any family idol worship by my parents in the name of Jesus.

34. I pull down the stronghold of satanic influence exercised upon my life by any other person in charge of me as an infant in the name of Jesus.

35. In Jesus' holy and mighty name, I break down the images of anestral god and I totally overthrow them and release myself from their domination and control forever.

36. In Jesus' name, I break every stronghold and fear of false gods in my life. I bind and cast out the spirit of fear, and the spirit of fear of revenge by false gods.

37. In the mighty name of Jesus, I command every spirit executing the curse of fear and untimely death against me to be bound and go to the place Jesus has prepared for them never to return.

38. Let the perfect love of Jesus which casts out fear enter into my life. I declare that God has not given me a spirit of fear but of love and power and a sound mind.

39. I break the curse of evil ritual covenant in Jesus' name.

40. I cut myself off from all cobra and serpentine worship, ancestral and otherwise in the name of Jesus.

Joshua prayed - sun stood still.

DEFEATING HOUSEHOLD WICKEDNESS

Scripture Reading for meditation: Genesis 37; Judges 15:9-13, Micah 7:6, Matt. 10:36
Confession: Revelation 13:10

PRAYER POINTS

1. Loving heavenly Father, I come to You in the name of my Saviour Jesus Christ.
2. I confess, renounce and repent of all my sins. *(Name sins as the Lord convicts you, audibly but quietly to Him.)*
3. I forgive every person who has hurt or sinned against me. Especially I forgive *(name those the Lord recalls to your mind who have damaged you in any hurtful way).*
4. I confess, renounce and repent from the sins of idolatry in my life, and in the life of my ancestors and forefathers, known and unknown in the name of Jesus.
5. I repent of personal and parental demonic guidance and astrological predictions over my life and I loose myself from every family demonic bondage to soothsayers and medicine men, mediums and sorcerers, withcdoctors and all ungodly men and women.
6. I loose myself from the evil effect of demonic birth chart made over my life in the name of Jesus.

Ere you left your room this morning, did you think to pray?

7. I repent of consumption and swallowing demonic materials and portions of medicine men by myself and my ancestors.

8. I repent of all serpent worship, and the worship of animal deities and forces of air, fire, water, and nature.

9. Forgive me and my ancestors, O Lord, of every form of idol worship, and every past agreement with any ungodly covenant set up by Satan and his demons over our lives in the name of Jesus.

10. I declare the sovereignty of the Lord Jesus Christ in my life and call upon Him to set me and my ancestral line free through the confession of my faith in Him alone.

11. I release myself from every unconscious ancestral bondage in the name of Jesus.

12. O Lord, make me a terror to household wickedness in the name of Jesus.

13. I withdraw the control of my life from the control and domination of household wickedness in the mighty name of Jesus.

14. I withdraw the programme of my life from the hands of household enemies in the mighty name of Jesus.

15. Let the joy of the enemy over my life be turned to sorrow in the name of Jesus.

16. I disgrace the strongman delegated by satan over my life in the name of Jesus.

17. I cut off any problem-inviting link with my parents in the name of Jesus.

18. Let every bondage of inherited sickness break in the name of Jesus.

19. I break every placental bondage in the name of Jesus.

20. I withdraw my future and progress from the influence and control of household wickedness in the mighty name of Jesus.

21. Let the fire of God destroy the habitations of evil remote controllers fashioned against my life in the name of Jesus.

When your heart was filled with anger, did you think to pray?

22. Let all evil tree planted against me be uprooted in the name of Jesus.
23. I command all spiritual vultures wishing for my death to receive the stones of fire in the mighty name of Jesus.
24. Let the Lord confuse the tongues of those gathered for my sake to do me harm after the order of the builders of the Tower of Babel in the name of Jesus.
25. Let my adversaries make mistakes that will advance my cause in the name of Jesus.
26. Let every evil tongue uttering unprofitable things about my life be completely silenced in the name of Jesus.
27. I command every evil power and vessels sitting on my rights and goodness to be violently over thrown in the name of Jesus.
28. I pursue, overtake and recover my properties from the hands of spiritual Egyptians in the name of Jesus.
29. Let every counsel, plan, desire, expectation, imagination, device and activity of the enemy against my life be rendered null and void in the name of Jesus.
30. I terminate every journey into bondage and unfruitfulness designed for me by the enemies of my soul in the name of Jesus.
31. I bind every money-consuming demon attached to my finances in the name of Jesus.
32. I refuse to be tossed around by any demonic device of the enemy to delay my miracle in the name of Jesus.
33. Let all satanic banks and purses receive the fire of God and burn to ashes in the name of Jesus.
34. Holy Spirit, teach me to avoid unfriendly friends and unprofitable transactions.
35. Let all my blessings presently in the prison of the enemy begin to pursue me and overtake me as from today in the name of Jesus.

When sore trials came upon you, did you think to pray?

36. Let the unprofitable chariot and riders be cast into dead sleep in the name of Jesus.

37. Let any evil sleep undertaken to harm me be converted to dead sleep in the name of Jesus.

38. Let all the weapons and devices of oppressors and tormentors fashioned against me be rendered impotent in the name of Jesus.

39. Let the Fire of God destroy any power operating spiritual vehicles working against me in the name of Jesus.

40. Let all evil advices given against my favour crash and disintegerate in the name of Jesus.

PRAY IN THE SPIRIT FOR 15 MINUTES. *(See note on how to use this book - page vi.)*

REMOVING UNFAVOURABLE LABELS AND REVERSING EVIL DESIGNS

Scripture Reading for meditation: Mark 10:46-52
Confession: Isaiah 64:1

PRAYER POINTS

Make this confessions boldly and loudly.

Jesus is Lord over my spirit, soul and body for the word of God tells me that at the name of Jesus, every knee shall bow. I can do all things through Christ who strengthens me. The Lord is my shepherd, I shall not want. God has delivered me from the powers of darkness and has translated me into the kingdom of His dear Son. In Jesus I have redemption through His shed blood and also forgiveness of sins. Jesus has blotted out the handwriting of ordinances that was against me which was contrary to me, and took it out of the way nailing it to His cross. I am the body of Christ. I am redeemed from the curse of the law because Jesus bore my physical and spiritual diseases in His body. I have the mind of Christ and hold the thoughts, feelings and purposes of His heart.

PRAYER POINTS

1. Thank the Lord for His power to deliver from any form of bondage.
2. I plead the blood of Jesus over my spirit, soul and body.

O how praying rests the weary!

3. Let every design against my life be completely nullified in the name of Jesus.

4. Let all evil labels fashioned by the camp of the enemy against my life be rubbed off by the blood of Jesus.

Sing the song "HOLY GHOST FIRE, FIRE FALL ON ME" with full concentration and in faith.

5. I vomit every satanic deposit in my life in the mighty name of Jesus. *(Prime the expulsion of these things by coughing slightly. Refuse to swallow any saliva coming out from the mouth.)*

6. I break myself loose from the bondage of stagnancy in the mighty name of Jesus.

7. Lord destroy with Your fire anything that makes Your promise to fail upon my life, no matter the origin.

As you pray No. 8, take 3-4 deep breaths determinedly expelling and flushing out spiritual contamination. Do so aggressively in the Mighty Name of Jesus.

8. Let the blood, the fire and the living water of the Most high God wash my system clean from:-
    a) Impurities acquired from parental contamination
    b) Evil spiritual consumptions
    c) Hidden sicknesses
    d) Remote control mechanisms
    e) Physical and spiritual incisions
    f) Satanic poisons
    g) Evil stamps, labels and links.

9. Let my body reject every evil habitation in the mighty name of our Lord Jesus Christ.

10. O Lord, enlarge my coast.

11. O Lord, reverse all evil arrangements attracted consciously or unconsciously to my life.

Prayer will change the night to day.

12. I reject all evil manipulations and manipulators in the mighty name of Jesus.
13. I break the power of the occult, witchcraft and familiar spirits over my life in the name of Jesus.
14. O Lord, ignite me with Holy Ghost Fire.

Prime the expulsion of the folowing things by heaving deeply and applying little force upon the lower part of the abdomen.

15. I deliver and pass out any satanic deposit in my intestine.
16. I deliver and pass out any satanic deposit in my reproductive organs.
17. *IN THE NAME OF JESUS, I DECLARE BEFORE ALL THE FORCES OF DARKNESS, "JESUS CHRIST IS LORD OVER EVERY DEPARTMENT OF MY LIFE".*
18. Holy Ghost Fire, do the work of purification in my life.
19. Lord Jesus, walk back through every second of my life to heal me and make me whole.
20. Lord Jesus, go back into the 3rd and 4th generation and break all unprofitable family ties.
21. Lord Jesus, set me free from any negative force transmitted to me in my mother's womb.
22. Lord Jesus, use Your spiritual eraser to wipe all painful and unprofitable memories from my mind.
23. Lord, repair any damage done to my spirit by satanic agents.
24. Let all covenants of failure in my life break in the name of Jesus.
25. I break all covenant bondages in the name of Jesus.
26. All the problems having to do with spiritual padlocks should receive divine solution in the name of Jesus.
27. Let all buried goodnesses and prosperities receive divine ressurection in Jesus' name.
28. All the problems associated with dead relatives should receive divine solution in Jesus' name.

So, when life seems dark and dreary, don't forget to pray.

29. All the problems associated with demonic in-laws should receive divine solution in Jesus' name.

30. All the problems associated with untimely death should receive divine solution in Jesus' name.

31. I refuse to turn back at the edge of victory in the name of Jesus.

32. Any problem associated with obtaining children from the wrong source should receive divine solution in Jesus' name.

33. Any problem originating from obtaining wife/husband from the wrong source should receive divine solution in Jesus' name.

34. All the problems originating from empty baskets should receive divine solution in Jesus' name.

35. Lord, deliver me from sin that easily besets.

36. Let every resistance to the moving of the Power of God be melted away by the fire of the Holy Ghost.

37. Let all the problems associated with physical or spiritual poison, receive divine solution in the name of Jesus.

38. Let all evil eyes observing my progress, be blinded in the name of Jesus.

39. All prayer obstructions and prayerlessness should depart in the name of Jesus.

40. Let my enemies begin to fall into their own traps in the name of Jesus.

CASTING OPPRESSORS INTO DEAD SLEEP

Scripture Reading for meditation: Psalm 118
Confession: Psalm 76:6

PRAYER POINTS

1. Let the stronghold of every spirit of Korah, Dathan and Abiram militating against me be cast down in the name of Jesus.
2. Let every spirit of Balaam hired to curse me fall after the order of Balaam in the name of Jesus.
3. Let every spirit of Sanballat and Tobiah planning evil against me receive the stones of fire in the name of Jesus.
4. Let every spirit of Egypt fall after the order of Pharoah in the name of Jesus.
5. Let every spirit of Herod receive the smite of angels in the name of Jesus.
6. Let every spirit of Goliath receive the stones of fire in the name of Jesus.
7. Let every spirit of Pharoah fall into the red sea in the name of Jesus.
8. Let all satanic mechanisms aimed at changing my destiny be frustrated in the name of Jesus.
9. Let every evil shadow be melted by the Holy Ghost fire.

Did you linger there, in prevailing prayer?

10. Let all unprofitable broadcasters of my goodness be silenced in Jesus' name.
11. Let all leaking bags and pockets be sealed up in the name of Jesus.
12. All evil monitoring gadgets fashioned against me, be swallowed in Jesus' name.
13. Let every evil effect of strange touches be removed from my life in the name of Jesus.
14. Let every blessing confiscated by witchcraft spirits be released in the name of Jesus.
15. Let every blessing confiscated by familiar spirits be released in the name of Jesus.
16. Let every blessing confiscated by ancestral spirits be released in the name of Jesus.
17. Let every blessing confiscated by envious enemies be released in the name of Jesus.
18. Let every blessing confiscated by satanic agents be released in the name of Jesus.
19. Let every blessing confiscated by principalities be released in the name of Jesus.
20. Let every blessing confiscated by rulers of darkness be released in the name of Jesus.
21. Let every blessing confiscated by evil powers be released in the name of Jesus.
22. Let all the blessings confiscated by spiritual wickedness in heavenly places be released in the name of Jesus.
23. Let all demonic reverse gears installed to hinder progress, be roasted in the name of Jesus.
24. Let the anointing of the overcomer fall upon me in Jesus' name.
25. Let all my Israel in bondage be released and let my Egypt be imprisoned in the name of Jesus.

Did you pray it through?

26. Let every unprofitable chariot and riders be cast into dead sleep in the name of Jesus.
27. Any evil sleep undertaken to harm me should be converted to dead sleep in the name of Jesus.
28. Let all weapons and devices of oppressors and tormentors be rendered impotent in the name of Jesus.
29. Let the Fire of God destroy the power operating any spiritual vehicle working against me in the name of Jesus.
30. Let all evil advices given against my favour crash and disintegerate in the name of Jesus.
31. I claim my divine promotion today in Jesus' name.
32. Lord, make me succeed and bring me into prosperity in the name of Jesus.
33. Promotion, progress and success are mine today in Jesus' name.
34. Let all the eaters of flesh and drinkers of blood, stumble and fall in the name of Jesus.
35. I command stubborn pursuers to pursue themselves in Jesus' name.
36. Let the wind, the sun and the moon run contrary to every demonic presence in my environment in the name of Jesus.
37. You devourers, vanish from my labour in the name of Jesus.
38. Let every tree planted by fear in my life dry up to the roots in the name of Jesus.
39. I cancel all enchantments, curses and spells that are against me in the name of Jesus.
40. Lord, use my life to confuse my enemies.

LET IT BE KNOWN THAT THOU ART GOD

Scripture Reading for meditation: 1 Kings 18
Confession: Psalm 20:7

PRAYER POINTS

1. Praise the Lord from the bottom of your heart for the miracles you have received since the beginning of this programme.
2. Father, let the windows of heaven open for me in the name of Jesus.
3. I command the ladder of the enemy into any department of my life to be broken to pieces in the name of Jesus.
4. I invite the spirit of confusion and division to come upon the forces of enemy in the name of Jesus.
5. I cancel all curses known or unknown uttered against me in the name of Jesus.
6. I loose myself from the bondage of fear in Jesus' name.
7. Let every tree planted by fear in my life dry up to the roots in the name of Jesus.
8. I command all evil spiritual marks to go in the mighty name of Jesus.
9. I nullify the activities and consequences of any evil thing I have tread upon in the name of Jesus.

At the place of prayer Jesus waits for you, did you meet Him there?

10. Lord, reverse every damage done to my life from the womb.
11. I break and release myself from every marital curse in the redemptive name of the Lord Jesus.
12. Lord make me a source of blessing to my family.
13. I bind and render to naught all evil counsels and imaginations against me in the name of Jesus.
14. I close entrance doors at poverty and close exit doors at blessings in the name of Jesus.
15. Lord, make my enemies to bow before me and congratulate me.
16. Lord, remove the garment of suffering as you did for Joseph.
17. Lord, remove the garment of sickness as you did for Hezekiah.
18. Lord, remove the garment of debt as you did for the widow through Elisha.
19. Lord, remove the garment of reproach as you did for Hannah.
20. Lord, remove the garment of death as you did for Shadrach.
21. Let all departed glory be restored in the mighty name of Jesus.
22. Let all captured blessings be released in the name of Jesus.
23. Let my blood reject the spirit of infirmity in the name of Jesus.
24. I command all invisible evil followers to be scattered in the name of Jesus.
25. Let God arise and all the forces of Pharoah scatter in the name of Jesus.
26. I release my life from any spiritual cage in the name of Jesus.
27. Let liquid fire pour down on all spiritual thieves in my life in the name of Jesus.
28. Let evil spiritual shoes burn to ashes in the name of Jesus.
29. Let evil spiritual foods dished against my life be consumed with liquid fire in the name of Jesus.

As the Master prayed in the garden alone, have you prayed it through?

30. Let the spirit of confusion depart from every department of my life in the name of Jesus.

31. All evil architects, cease your evil construction works in my life in the name of Jesus.

32. Let all attacks by evil night creatures be neutralized in the name of Jesus.

33. Let all the trees habouring hidden blessings of God's children release their captives in the name of Jesus.

34. Every gathering held in the air, land, water, forest, contrary to my life should be scattered in the name of Jesus.

35. Let the evil mouths speaking against me fall after the order of Balaam in the name of Jesus.

36. Let all antagonistic parents and in-laws receive divine touch in the name of Jesus.

37. Let every effect of any strange handshake and kiss be nullified in the name of Jesus.

38. Let all powers that are after my life stumble and fall in the name of Jesus.

39. Lord, let promotions and miracles galore overshadow my life.

40. Let every evil effect of contaminated underwears, be repaired in the name of Jesus.

41. I disengage my blessings from the hands of the devourers in the name of Jesus.

42. I disengage my business from the hands of the emptiers in the name of Jesus.

43. I disengage my wife/husband from the hands of the powers that put asunder in the name of Jesus.

44. O Lord, deliver me from the powers that waste divine opportunity.

45. O Lord, cause me to become undeafeatable by the tentacles of temptations.

Did you plead in the Saviour's name?

46. O Lord, place me on the mountain of glory and power.
47. Lord, make the Mountain of Fire and Miracles a citadel of signs, wonders, miracles, outstanding conversions and holiness.
48. Thank the Lord for answered prayers.

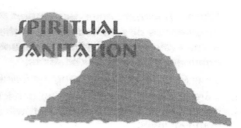

SPIRITUAL SANITATION

88

Scripture Reading: *Psalm 139*
Confession: *Psalm 139:23*

PRAYER POINTS

1. *Take a piece of paper and a pen.*
2. *Pray aggressively that the Holy Spirit will reveal your real self to you. Promise the Lord that you will be hard and honest on yourself.*
3. *Now begin to make a list of specific areas in your life where brokeness is not perfect e.g.*

    "Ocassional lying"

    "I still exhibit traits of unholy anger"

    "Sexual thoughts", etc.
4. *Remember to add all bad habits still present in your life. Take time to do this thoroughly leaving no stones untouched. Any cover-up will only give the enemy a legal ground to stay longer. Spend time before the Lord to declare war on the weaknesses in your life. Remember that the food of the strongman and his stronghold is your weaknesses.*
5. *Now make the following confessions.*

    God has delivered me from the power of darkness and has translated me into the kingdom of His dear Son Jesus

---

The motion of a hidden fire, that trembles in the breat.

Christ. In whom I have redemption through His blood, the forgiveness of sins according to the riches of His Grace. He has raised me together and made me to sit together in heavenly places in Christ Jesus.

Now Pray aggressively using the following prayer points.

6. I break myself loose from any conscious and unconscious bondage hindering my spiritual growth and development in the name of Jesus.

7. Let every negative anointing depart from my life in the mighty name of Jesus.

8. Father, re-organise my life according to Your will in the name of Jesus.

9. Father, repair the good things in my life that I have destroyed with my own hands in the name of Jesus.

10. Holy Ghost Fire, do the work of purification in my life.

11. Lord Jesus, walk back through every second of my life to heal me and make me whole.

12. Lord Jesus, go back into the 3rd and 4th generation and break all unprofitable family ties.

13. Lord Jesus, set me free from any negative force transmitted to me in my mother's womb.

14. Lord Jesus, use Your spiritual eraser to wipe all painful and unprofitable memories from my mind.

15. Every resistance to the moving of the Power of God in my life should be melted away by the fire of the Holy Spirit in the name of Jesus.

16. Make me a pillar in Your house, O God.

17. Father, crucify anything in me that would remove my name from the book of life.

18. Father, help me to crucify my flesh in the name of Jesus.

19. If my name has been removed from the book of life, Father, re-write my name in the name of Jesus.

Prayer is the simplest form of speech, that infant lips can try.

20. Lord, give me power to overcome myself.

21. I confess, repent and renouce the sin of unforgiveness, of allowing bad memories to poison my heart and my thoughts, of spiritual laziness and being insensitive to the Holy Spirit.

22. O Lord, cleanse my mind of every sinful and destructive memory.

23. O Lord, cleanse my heart and renew a right spirit within me that I might walk free of all sins.

24. *Spend quality time to stand against the spirits listed hereunder. Pray aggressively as follows;*

    "You spirit of . . ., loose your hold upon my life in the name of Jesus. I command you to be separated from me. I place the cross of Jesus between me and you. I forbid you to ever return or ever to send any other spirits in the mighty name of Jesus".

    TAKE EACH SPIRIT ONE AT A TIME AND BE VIOLENT. If you notice any reaction, stop and deal thoroughly with it before you proceed to the next point.

    1. Self deception
    2. Childish self-will
    3. Pride
    4. Despair
    5. Hopelessness
    6. Death
    7. Confusion
    8. Rejection
    9. Infirmity
    10. Religion
    11. Vagabond
    12. Impatience
    13. False vision
    14. Arrested development
    15. Covetiousness
    16. Greediness
    17. Depression
    18. Torment
    19. Doubt
    20. Fear
    21. Anger
    22. Contention
    23. Resentment
    24. Bitterness
    25. Criticism
    26. Foolishness
    27. Addiction
    28. Lust
    29. Cowardice
    30. Terror

Prayer is the sublimest strains that reach the majesty on high.

31. Inferiority
32. Leviathan
33. Frustration
34. Forgetfulness
35. False front
36. Enchantment
37. Temper
38. Condemnation
39. Unforgiveness
40. Filthy conversation
41. Dirty dreams
42. Filthy imagination
43. Cruelty
44. Deformity
45. Legalism
46. UnGodly ambition for recognition
47. Lust and ambition for power and control in religious matters
48. Helplessness
49. Failure
50. Heaviness
51. Vanity
52. Strife
53. Waste
54. False compassion

25. Thank the Lord for answered prayers.

Prayer is the contrite sinner's voice, returning from his ways.

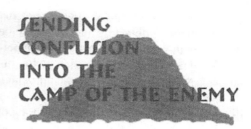

JENDING CONFUJION INTO THE CAMP OF THE ENEMY

Scripture Reading : Psalm 109
Confession : Jer. 20:11

PRAYER POINTS

1. Let all the powers encamping against my goodness and breakthroughs become confused and be scatterred in the name of Jesus.
2. Let all the powers of my adversaries be rendered impotent in the name of Jesus.
3. Let every evil tongue uttering curses and other evil pronouncements against my life be completely silenced in the name of Jesus.
4. I command every evil stronghold and powers housing my rights and goodness to be violently overthrown in the name of Jesus.
5. I pursue, overtake and recover my properties from the hands of spiritual robbers in the name of Jesus.
6. Let every counsel, plan, desire, expectation, imagination, device and activity of the oppressors against my life be rendered null and void in the name of Jesus.
7. I terminate every contract and cancel every evil promisory notes kept in satanic files for my sake in the name of Jesus.
8. I release myself fom the powers and activities of the wasters in the name of Jesus.

While angels in their songs rejoice, and say, "Behold, he prays".

9. I refuse to be tossed around by any evil remote control device fashioned to delay my miracle in the name of Jesus.
10. Let all the citadels of evil summoning of the spirit receive the fire of God and burn to ashes in the name of Jesus.
11. Holy Spirit, teach me to avoid unfriendly foods and unprofitable discussions.
12. Let all my goodness presently in the prison of the enemy begin to pursue me and overtake me as from today in the name of Jesus.
13. Let all strange fire prepared against my life be quenched in the name of Jesus.
14. I command every tongue issuing destruction against me to be condemned in the name of Jesus.
15. Let all the troublers of my Israel be disbanded and confused in the name of Jesus.
16. Let the Blood of Jesus clean off all unprofitable marks in any department of my life.
17. Let all strange hands that have touched my blood be neutralised in the name of Jesus.
18. I command the spirit that abandons blessings to be bound in the name of Jesus.
19. I receive victory over the host of wickedness surrounding me in the name of Jesus.
20. I stand against dream defeats and its effects in the name of Jesus.
21. Let every spirit attacking me in the form of animals receive the fire of God.
22. I stand against the operations of the spirit of death in my life in the name of Jesus.
23. Let the counsel of the devil against me be destroyed and be frustrated in the name of Jesus.

Prayer is the christian's vital breath, the christian's native air.

24. I bind the spirit of doubt, unbelief, fear and tradition in the name of Jesus.

25. Father, destroy every stronghold of the powers of darkness in my family in the name of Jesus.

26. Let every problem affecting the brain, be neutralised in the name of Jesus.

27. Let every evil effect of ritual killing upon my life by ancestors be neutralised in the name of Jesus.

28. Let all terminal, genetic, and ancestral sicknesses be healed in the name of Jesus.

29. Lord give me power to pursue and overtake the enemy and also to recover my stolen property.

30. O God, Let Your fire destroy every foundational problem in my life in the name of Jesus.

31. Let every link, label and stamp of the oppressors be destroyed by the blood of Jesus.

32. Every evil spiritual pregnancy in my life, be aborted in the name of Jesus.

33. Let every dirty hands be removed from the affairs of my life in the name of Jesus.

34. Let every effect of evil access to my blood be reversed now in the name of Jesus.

35. Let everything done against me under the devil's anointing be neutralized now in the name of Jesus.

36. All evil vessels dispatched to do me harm should crash in the name of Jesus.

37. Satanic banks, release my properties in your hand in Jesus' name.

38. I remove my name from the book of untimely death in the name of Jesus.

39. I remove my name from the book of tragedy in Jesus' name.

His watchword at the gate of death; He enters heaven with prayer.

40. All evil umbrellas preventing heavenly showers from falling upon me, be roasted in the name of Jesus.
41. Let all evil associations summoned for my sake be scattered in the name of Jesus.
42. Let every problem connected to polygamy in my life, be nullified in Jesus' name.
43. I command every satanic reinforcement against me to scatter in the name of Jesus.
44. I cancel all evil vows that are affecting me negatively in the name of Jesus.
45. I destroy the clock and the time-table of the enemy for my life in the name of Jesus.
46. Lord, reschedule my enemies to useless and harmless assignments.
47. Let every evil device against me be disappointed in Jesus' name.
48. Let the Healing power of the Holy Spirit, overshadow me.
49. I bind every spirit working against answers to my prayers in the name of Jesus.
50. I disarm any power that has made a covenant with the ground, water and wind about me in the name of Jesus.
51. O Lord, make my life invisible to demonic observers.
52. I bind all evil remote control spirits in the name of Jesus.
53. I withdraw all the bullets and ammunition made available to the enemy in the name of Jesus.
54. I revoke any conscious or unconscious covenant with the spirit of death in the name of Jesus.
55. In the name of Jesus, I call on the heavenly surgeon to perform surgical operations where necessary in my life.
56. I refuse to be spiritually amputated in the name of Jesus.
57. I refuse to wage war against myself in the name of Jesus.
58. O Lord, wake me up from any form of spiritual sleep.

Have you discovered the treasure and happiness in prayer?

59. All evil seeds planted by fear into my life should be uprooted in the name of Jesus.
60. Father of our Lord Jesus Christ, let Your Kingdom be established in every area of my life.
61. I cancel all former negotiations with the devil in Jesus' name.
62. Let all my buried goodness and prosperity receive divine ressurection in Jesus' name.
63. I refuse to turn back at the edge of victory in the name of Jesus.
64. Father, pour out shame on all the powers struggling to put me to shame in the name of Jesus.
65. Let all drinkers of blood and eaters of flesh turn on themselves in the name of Jesus.
66. Spiritual problems attached to months: January, February, March, April, May, June, July, August, September, October, November, December, be nullified in the name of Jesus.
67. O Lord deliver me from all coldness of heart and weakness of will.
68. O Lord, let my life shine the light of goodness and love.
69. O Lord, let my will be lost in Your will
70. Pray in the spirit for 10 minutes. *(See note on how to use this book - page vi.)*

Do you know it's prayer that takes one to the Father's bossom?

FINDING FAVOUR WITH OTHERS

Confession

Deut 28:13: *And the LORD shall make thee the head, and not the tail; and thou shalt be above only, and thou shalt not be beneath; if that thou hearken unto the commandments of the LORD thy God, which I command thee this day, to observe and to do them.*

Prov 21:1: *The king's heart is in the hand of the LORD, as the rivers of water: he turneth it whithersoever he will.*

Prov 11:27: *He that diligently seeketh good procureth favour: but he that seeketh mischief, it shall come unto him.*

Zech 12:10: *And I will pour upon the house of David, and upon the inhabitants of Jerusalem, the spirit of grace and of supplications: and they shall look upon me whom they have pierced, and they shall mourn for him, as one mourneth for his only son, and shall be in bitterness for him, as one that is in bitterness for his firstborn.*

Ps 8:5: *For thou hast made him a little lower than the angels, and hast crowned him with glory and honour.*

Eph 3:19-20: *And to know the love of Christ, which passeth knowledge, that ye might be filled with all the fulness of God. Now unto him that is able to do exceeding abundantly above all that we ask or think, according to the power that worketh in us.*

Ps 30:5: *For his anger endureth but a moment; in his favour is life: weeping may endure for a night, but joy cometh in the morning.*

Prayer people are happy people.

Dan 1:9: *Now God had brought Daniel into favour and tender love with the prince of the eunuchs.*

PRAYER POINTS

1. Father, make all my proposals to find favour in the sight of . . . in the name of Jesus.
2. Lord, let me find favour ,compassion and loving-kindnes with . . . concerning this business.
3. Let all the demonic obstacles that has been established in the heart of . . . against my prosperity be destroyed in Jesus' name.
4. Lord, show . . . dreams, visions and restlessness that would advance my cause.
5. I command my money being caged by the enemy to be completely released in the name of Jesus.
6. Lord, give me supernatural breakthroughs in all my present business proposals.
7. I bind and put to flight all the spirits of fear, anxiety and discouragement in the name of Jesus.
8. Lord, let divine wisdom fall upon all who are supporting me in these matters.
9. I break the backbone of any further spirits of conspiracy and treachery in the name of Jesus.
10. Lord, hammer my matter into the mind of those who will assist me so that they do not suffer from demonic loss of memory.
11. I paralyse the handiwork of house hold enemies and envious agents in this matter in the name of Jesus.
12. You devil take your legs away from the top of my finances in the mighty name of Jesus.
13. Let the fire of the Holy spirit purge my life from any evil mark put upon me in the name of Jesus.
14. Thank the Lord for answered prayers.

Prayer people are hell-shaker people.

PRAYERS TO UNCAGE PARTNER

AGGRESSIVE CONFESSION

The word of God says I shall decree a thing and it shall be estab-
lished. I decree that my partner be released from any anti-marriage
or divorce cage in the mighty name of the Lord Jesus Christ. What
God has joined together, let no man put asunder. I command all
the forces battling against my home be completly uprooted for they
are trying to put asunder what God has joined together. I tread over
serpent and scorpions in the mighty name of Jesus. Let the angels
of the living God pursue the architects of anti-marriage cages in the
mighty name of Jesus.

PRAYER POINTS

1. I command every spirit of division to depart from my marital life in the name of Jesus.
2. You spirit of Egypt, release my . . . in the name of Jesus.
3. Let all family cages holding my . . . receive the fire of God.
4. Lord Jesus wash away all anti-marriage stamps, labels and links in the mighty name of Jesus.
5. Let the spirit of love and understanding prevail within us in the name of Jesus.
6. Let every demonic family interference be completely severed in the name of Jesus.

Prayer people are the beloved of the Father.

7. Holy Spirit, overshadow this relationship.
8. I command all stubborn yokes to break in the name of Jesus.
9. Let all the effects of spiritual wedding rings, clothes and shoes be completely removed in the name of Jesus.
10. I bind all the stubborn pursuers militating against my home in the mighty name of Jesus.
11. I command the veil of hatred against me in the heart of . . . to be destroyed in the name of Jesus.
12. Let the wicked spirits polluting the heart of my . . . against me receive the stones of fire in the name of Jesus.
13. You . . . receive your divine senses back in the mighty name of Jesus.
14. O Lord, put the love for me back in the heart of my . . .
15. O lord reveal to me every other secret that I need to know concerning this problem.
16. Let the joy of the enemy on my home be converted to sorrow in the mighty name of Jesus.
17. You . . . you will not follow the evil patterns of any parent or ancestor in the name of Jesus.
18. Let all activities of spirits from the air, water, land and family idols loose their hold upon my marriage.
20. Let all activities contrary to marriage vows in the life of . . . be paralysed in the name of Jesus.
21. Let all spirits of fear, depression, worry and despair release me in the name of Jesus.

Do you know it's prayer that makes the world a living today - even as it is now?

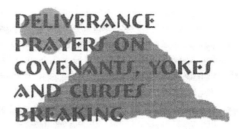

DELIVERANCE
PRAYERS ON
COVENANTS, YOKES
AND CURSES
BREAKING

Confession: Col. 2:14, Gal. 3: 13 & 14, 2 Cor. 6 14 - 18, Gal. 6:17, 2 Cor. 5:17

PRAYER POINTS
A.   RENOUNCING MEMBERSHIP OF EVIL ASSOCIATIONS

1. I reject, revoke and renounce my membership of any of the following evil associations.

    Jezebel spirit, Marine spirits, Water spirit, Queen of the Coast, Mermaid spirits, Familiar spirits, Witches and Wizards, Spirits of the dead and all other occult societies in the name of Jesus.

2. I withdraw and cancel my name from their registers with the blood of Jesus.

3. I reject and renounce all such names given to me in any of the evil associations in the name of Jesus.

4. I resign my position in any of these associations and withdraw my services and responsibilities permanently in the name of Jesus.

5. I reject all the evil works I have done to innocent people through my membership with these evil   association and beg the Almighty God to forgive me and wash me clean with the blood of Jesus.

6. I purge myself of all evil foods I had eaten in any of the evil associations with the blood of Jesus.

Prayer holds life and put it on the Father's bossom.

7. I bind you water spirits, marine, queen of the coast, Jezebel spirits, familiar spirits operating in my life with hot chains and fetters of God and cast you out into the deep, and seal you with unquenchable fire of God in the name of Jesus.

8. I withdraw any part of my body and blood deposited on the evil altars in the name of Jesus.

9. I withdraw my pictures, image and inner-man from the altars and covers of the evil associations in the name of Jesus.

10. I return any of the things of evil associations I am connected with, the instruments and any other properties at my disposal for the execution of duties in the name of Jesus.

11. I hereby confess total separation from the evil associations in the name of Jesus.

12. Holy Spirit, build a wall of fire round me that will completely make it not possible for these evil spirits to come to me again.

13. I break any covenant binding me with any of these evil associations in name of Jesus.

14. I break all inherited covenants and all such covenants I consciously and unconsciously entered into in the name of Jesus.

15. I bind the demons attached to these covenants and cast them into the deep in the name of Jesus..

16. I resist every attempt to return me back to the evil associations with the blood of Jesus, fire, brimstone and thunder of God.

17. I renounce and revoke all the oaths I took while entering the evil associations in the name of Jesus.

18. I break and cancel every evil mark, incision, writing placed in my spirit and body as a result of my membership of the evil associations with the blood of Jesus and purify my body, soul and spirit with the Holy Ghost Fire in the name of Jesus.

19. I break all covenants inherited from my ancestors on the father and mother side in the name of Jesus.

Let prayer change you.

20. Lord break down every evil foundation of my life and rebuild a new one on Christ the Rock.

21. I command the fire of God to roast and burn to ashes every evil bird, snake, or any other animal attached to my life by the evil association in the name of Jesus.

22. I dismantle every hinderance, obstacle or blockage put in my way of progress by my involvement in these evil associations in the name of Jesus.

23. All the doors of blessings and break-through shut against me due to my involvement in these evil associations, I command you to open in the name of Jesus.

B. CURSES

1. I break and cancel every inherited curse in the name of Jesus.

2. Lord remove from me all the curses placed upon my ancestral families as a result of their evil associations involvement in the name of Jesus.

3. I break and cancel every curse placed upon me by my parents in the name of Jesus.

4. I break and cancel every curse, spell, gannet, hex, enchantment, bewitchment, incantation placed upon me by my involvement with evil association in the name of Jesus.

5. I break and revoke every blood and soul-tie covenant and yokes attached to them in the name of Jesus.

6. I purge myself of all the evil foods I have eaten in the evil world with the blood of Jesus and purify myself with the fire of the Holy Ghost in the name of Jesus.

7. All demonic spirits attached to all these covenants and curses, be roasted with the fire of God in the name of Jesus.

8. I declare my body, soul and spirit a-no-go-area for all evil spirits in the name of Jesus.

Empty your heart to God in prayer and stop moving about with heavy loads.

C. DELIVERANCE PRAYERS FROM SPIRIT HUSBAND OR WIFE.

1. I divorce and renounce my marriage with the spirit husband or wife in the name of Jesus.
2. I break all covenants entered into with the spirit husband or wife in the name of Jesus.
3. I command the thunder fire of God to burn to ashes the wedding gown, ring, photographs and all other materials used for the marriage in the name of Jesus.
4. I send the fire of God to burn to ashes the marriage certificate in the name of Jesus.
5. I break every blood and soul-tie covenants with the spirit husband or wife in the name of Jesus.
6. I send thunder fire of God to burn to ashes the children born to the marriage in the name of Jesus.
7. I withdraw my blood, sperm or any other part of my body deposited in the altar of the spirit husband or wife in the name of Jesus.
8. I bind you spirit husband or wife tormenting my life and earthly marriage with hot chains and fetters of God and cast you out of my life in the depth pit and command you not to ever come into my life again in the name of Jesus.
9. I return to you every of your property in my possession in the spirit world including the dowry and whatsoever was used for the marriage and covenants in the name of Jesus.
10. I drain myself of all evil materials deposited in my body as a result of our sexual relation with the blood of Jesus.
11. Lord, send Holy Ghost fire into my root and burn out all unclean things deposited in it by the spirit husband and wife in the name of Jesus.
12. I break the head of snake deposit in the by the spirit husband

or wife to do me harm and command you to come out in the name of Jesus.

13. I purge out with the blood of Jesus every evil material deposited in my womb to prevent me from having children on earth.

14. Lord repair and restore every damage done to any part of my body and my earthly marriage by the spirit husband or wife in the name of Jesus.

15. I reject and cancel every curse, evil pronouncement, spell, jinx, enchantment and incantation placed upon me by the spirit husband or wife in the name of Jesus.

16. I take back and possess all my earthly belongings in the custody of the spirit husband or wife in the name of Jesus.

17. I command the spirit husband or wife to permanently turn his or her back on me forever in the name of Jesus.

18. I renounce and reject the name given to me by the spirit husband or wife in the name of Jesus.

19. I hereby declare and confess that the Lord Jesus Christ is my Husband till eternity in the name of Jesus.

20. I soak myself in the blood of Jesus and cancel the evil mark or writings placed on me in the name of Jesus.

21. I set myself free from the stronghold and domineering power and bondage of the spirit husband or wife in the name of Jesus.

22. I paralyse the remote control power and work used to destabilise my earthly marriage to hinder my child bearing for my earthly husband or wife in the name of Jesus.

D. COVENANTS AND YOKES BREAKING

1. I break every evil covenant with water spirits and the yokes attached to it in the name of Jesus.

2. I break and cancel every covenant with any idol and the yokes attached to it in the name of Jesus.

3. I break and cancel any evil covenant entered into by my parents on my behalf and all the yokes attached to it in the name of Jesus.

4. I command the fire of God to roast the forces of hinderance and obstacles and paralyse the power in the name of Jesus.

5. Lord, let the Holy Ghost effect immediate breakthrough in every area of my life in the name of Jesus.

6. I confess that my deliverance shall remain permanent never to be reversed again in the name of Jesus.

SCRIPTURES

A. DELIVERANCE

Exodus 15:6, Psalm 91:3, Psalm 107:6, Psalm 107:20, John 8:32, John 8:36

B. DELIVERANCE FOR ALCOHOLICS

Psalm 107:20, II Cor. 2:14, I John 3:8

C. DELIVERANCE FOR SMOKERS

Psalm 31:1-5, Psalm 31:7, Psalm 46:1, Psalm 55:18, Psalm 46:5, Psalm 107:6, Prov. 3:26, Prov. 26:11, Isa. 41:13, Rom. 8:32, I Cor. 3:16-17, Phil. 4:7, I John 3:8b

PRAYER POINTS

1. Father, I confess that, in the past, I had held unforgiveness, sometime bitterness and resentment in my heart against certain people who had hurt or disappointed me.

2. I now recognise this as a sin and confess it as sin, for You have said in Your Word that if we confess our sin, You are faithful and just to forgive us our sin and to cleanse us of all un-righteousness (1 John 1:9).

3. I do now forgive the following people, whom I can remember, who have hurt or disappointed me. *(Mention names of those who come to your mind.)* I now freely forgive all these people

---

Prayer makes a history of wonders

and ask You to bless them if they are living.

4. I also forgive myself for all my many faults and failures, for You have freely forgiven me.

5. Thank You Father for freedom from the load of unforgiveness, bitterness and resentment in Jesus' name.

6. Father, I confess to You, that in the past, through ignorance, through curiosity or through wilfulness, I have come into contact with certain sinful acts. I now recognise this as sin and confess it as sin, claiming forgiveness in the name of Jesus.

7. Specifically, I do confess as sin and renounce all contacts which I have had with the following occult things: (*here mention every thing in the occult category with which you have dabbled or become involved*).

8. I also renounce and confess as sin any oath which I have made to any false god and any idolatry in which I have been involved.

9. Satan, I rebuke you in the name of Jesus, and I am closing any door which I or my ancestors may have opened to you and your demons in the name of Jesus.

10. I renounce satan and all his demons, I declare them to be my enemies and I command them out of my life completely in the name of Jesus.

11. In the name of Jesus Christ, I now claim deliverance from any and all evil spirits which may be in me (Joel 2:28). Once and for all, I close the door in my life to all occult practices and command all related spirits to leave me now in the name of Jesus.

12. I the name of Jesus, I break any curse of rejection from the womb or illegitimacy which may be in my family, even back to ten generations on both sides of the family (Deut. 26:2).

13. In the name of Jesus, I now renounce, break and loose myself from all demonic subjection and from any ungodly soul ties to my mother, father, grandparents or any other person, living or dead, who have ever dominated or controlled me in any way

---

which is contrary to the will of God and God's Word.

14. I also repent and ask You to forgive me, if I have ever dominated or controlled some other person in the wrong way.

15. In the name of Jesus Christ, I now renounce, break and loose myself and all descendants from all psychic heredity, demonic holds, psychic powers, bondage, bonds of physical or mental illness, or curses which may be upon my family line as a result of sins, transgressions, iniquities, occult or psychic involvements of myself, my parents, or any of my ancestors, (my spouse, any and all ex spouses, or their parents, or any of their ancestors).

16. In the name of Jesus Christ, I now renounce, break and loose myself and all my descendants from all evil curses, charms, vexes, spells, jinxes, psychic powers, bewitchments, witchcraft or sorcery which may have been put upon me or my family line; from any person or persons; or from any occult or psychic source. I renounce all connected and related spirits and command them to leave me now.

17. I thank You Lord Jesus for setting me free.

18. In the name of Jesus Christ, I command Satan and all of his demons to loose my mind completely.

19. I ask You Father to send Your angels to break, cut and sever all fetters, bands, chains, and ties and bonds of whatever sort the enemy has managed to place on my mind, by word or deed.

20. I ask You to loose into me and my family the spirits of the Lord: wisdom, counsel, might, knowledge, fear of the Lord, power, love, sound mind, grace, peace and the spirit of the Lord.

21. Father, I break and renounce, cut and break all evil soul ties which I may have with lodges, religious systems, adulterers, drunkards, drug addicts, close friends, cult, etc.

22. Father, I ask You in the name of Jesus Christ to send Your angels to gather up the fragments of my soul and restore them

to their rightful place in me. Have them unearth and break all earthen storage vessels; also all bonds; bands or binding which have been put upon my soul by any means.

23. I claim the restoration of my soul.

24. Let all the pieces of my fragmented mind, will, and emotions be brought back into proper and original positions where they belong.

25. In the name of Jesus Christ, I break any and all curses placed against me by witchcraft and command that those curses and spirits from them return to the senders (Psalm 109:17,18).

26. In accord with Leviticus 26, I do now confess the sins of my ancestors: idolatry, witchcraft, occultism, lust, adultery, divorce, perversion, pride unbelief, rebellion, stubbornness.

27. I claim forgiveness because of the provisions in 1John 1:9, declare the curses broken and lift the curses, whoredoms and iniquities from me and my descendants.

28. I command all connected and related spirits to leave me and my family and go wherever Jesus wants them to go.

29. I confess that my body is the temple of the Holy Spirit: redeemed, cleansed, and sanctified by the blood of Jesus Christ. Therefore, Satan has no more place in me, no more power over me, because of the blood of Jesus.

30. Satan, in the name of Jesus Christ the son of God, I put you and all your legions on notice that I am attacking you from my position in Christ at the right hand of the Father in the third heaven. This places me high above you, your principalities, power, thrones, dominions, world rulers, rulers of darkness, kings, princes and every angelic rank under your command.

    Romans 8:15: For I did not receive a spirit that makes one a slave again to fear (bondage); but I received the Spirit of sonship (adoption). And by Him I cry, "Abba, Father,"

31. *Call the spirit you do not desire in your life by name. Then issue*

God sometimes compels us to pray hard for the best things

the command firmly and repeatedly that the spirits must come out in the name of the Lord Jesus.

Pray as follows: You spirit of . . . ,

Addiction to, or craving for:

- Acid	- Caffeine	- LSD	- Peyote
- Alcohol	- Diet Pills	- Marijuana	- Speed
- Amphetamines	- Downers	- Methadone	
- STP	- Any drug	- ˙Hashish	
- Methedrine™	- Sugar	- Aspirin	- Heroine
- Mood elevators	- Tranquilizers	- Barbiturates	
- Junk food	- Nicotine . . .		

in belly, in blood, in lungs, in mind, in sinuses, in throat in the name of Jesus.

(Gluttony)

- Binge	- Greediness	- Nervousness
- Bulimia	- Moodiness	- Resentment
- Compulsiveness	- Self-reward	- Restlessness
- Frustration	- Sweet tooth	- Self-pity

Come out of my brain and mind in the name of Jesus.

32. I loose myself from you in the name of Jesus, and I command you to leave me right now in the mighty name of our Lord Jesus Christ.

DEFEATING
ANTI-HARVEST
FORCES

94

SCRIPTURES: *Mt . 12:28, Lk. 9:1 -2, Lk. 10:19, Acts 10:38, Mt. 8:16, Gen. 1:3, Jn. 1:1, Mk. 11:23, Ps. 107:2, Mt. 8: 28-34, Mt. 12:29, Mt. 16:19, Rm. 10:10, Rm. 10:17, Ps. 17:4, Jn. 14:23, Jn. 15:7-8, Isa. 65:22*

PRAYER POINTS

1. I stand against the following powers in the mighty name of Jesus.
    (a) The power to sow but not to reap.
    (b) The power to reap but not enjoy the fruits of one's labour
    (c) The powers of the emptier
    (d) The harvest consumers
    (e) The powers of the wasters
    (f) The spirit of financial and family destruction
2. Let all household wickedness be put to flight in Jesus' name.
3. Let all anti-glory forces loose their hold upon my life in the name of Jesus
4. I release myself from the bondage of leaking pockets in the name of Jesus
5. Let the following occurrences be paralysed in my life in the name of Jesus
    (a) Slippery blessings

There is a difference between faith in prayer and prayer in faith.

(b) Spiritual vulnerability

(c) Evil magnets

(d) Failure at the edge of miracles

(e) Evil pursuers

(f) Arrows of doubt

(g) Jungle spirit

6. I refuse to labour in vain in the name of Jesus

7. Father, make all proposals to find favour in the sight of men

8. Lord, let me find favour, compassion and loving-kindness with this Business

9. Let all the demonic obstacles that has been established in the heart of anyone against my prosperity be destroyed in the name of Jesus.

10. Lord, show me dreams and vision that would advance my cause.

11. I command my money being caged by the enemy to be completely released in the name of Jesus.

12. Lord give me supernatural breakthroughs in all my present business proposals.

13. I bind and put to flight all the spirits of fear, anxiety and discouragement in the name of Jesus.

14. Lord, let divine wisdom fall upon all who are supporting me in my endeavours

15. I break the backbone of any further spirit of conspiracy and treachery in the name of Jesus.

16. Lord, hammer my matter into the mind of those who will assist me so that they do not suffer from demonic loss of memory.

17. I paralyse the handiwork of household enemies and envious agents in my life in the name of Jesus

18. You devil take your legs away from the top of my finances in the name of Jesus.

19. Let the fire of Holy Spirit purge my life from any evil mark put upon me in the name of Jesus.

20. Thank the Lord for answered prayers.

REMOVING BLOCKAGES OPERATING AT THE EDGE OF MIRACLES

PRAYER POINTS

1. I confess my sins of exhibiting occasional doubts.
2. Let the Angels of the living God roll away the stone blocking my financial, physical and spiritual breakthroughs in the name of Jesus.
3. I bind every spirit manipulating my beneficiaries against me in the name of Jesus.
4. I remove my name from the book of seers of goodness without appropriation in the name of Jesus.
5. Let God arise and let all the enemies of my breakthrough be scattered in the name of Jesus.
6. Let the Fire of God melt away the stones hindering my blessings in the mighty name of Jesus.
7. Let the cloud blocking the sunlight of my glory and breakthrough be dispersed in Jesus' name.
8. All secrets of the enemy in the camp of my life that are still in the darkness, let them be revealed to me from now in the name of Jesus.
9. All evil spirits masquerading to trouble me, be bound in the name of Jesus.
10. Lord, let me not put unprofitable and heavy load upon myself in the name of Jesus.

Too many prayers are earthbound.

11. All keys to my goodness that are still in the possession of the enemy, Lord, give them unto me.

12. Open my eyes O Lord, and let my ways get not darkened before me.

13. All my sweat on the affairs of my life will not be in vain in the name of Jesus.

14. The pregnancy of good things within me will be not be aborted by any contrary power in the name of Jesus.

15. Lord, turn me to untouchable coals of fire.

16. Lord, let wonderful changes begin to be my lot from this week.

17. Lord, remove covetousness from my eyes.

18. Lord, fill the cup of my life to the brim.

19. Let every power stepping on my goodness receive the arrow of fire of God now in the name of Jesus.

20. I reject every spirit of the tail in all areas of my life in the name of Jesus.

21. Thank God for the victory.

Prayer is the means through which God releases power.

CONFESSION AND PRAYER FOR SUPERNATURAL CONCEPTION

96

CONFESSIONS: Deuteronomy 7:13-15, Exod. 23:25-26, Ps. 91:10, Ps. 113:9, Ps. 127:3-5, Ps. 128:3, Mal. 3:10-11

"Father, we thank You that children are the heritage of the Lord, and the fruit of the womb is His reward. Children are Your idea Father; You thought up children, and family and home. You instituted the family in the Garden of Eden. You ordered children; You commanded them when You said to Adam and Eve, "Be friutful and multiply". You said that the barren womb is never satisfied. Lord, the Word declares that I am wonderful and fearfully made by You; therefore, I'm perfect and able to conceive and have children. You said that I/ (my wife) would be a fruitful vine by the side of our house and our children like olive plants around our table. We are not ashamed but happy because our quiver is full of children (or arrows, as You call them).

"Thank You, Father, that You designed and fashoned me/her, to have children, that in the Bible barrenness was the exception, not the rule, not Your will, not normal, somethings against Your plan and purpose. And in Your goodness and faithfulness, every barren woman in the Bible who was godly and believed Your Word became pregnant; You opened her womb abd blessed her, and she gave birth to a precious baby just as I/she will. You make the barren woman to keep house and to be a joyful mother of children."

Prayer opened the red sea.

"You said, Father, that because You are our God and we are Your people and have a covenant with You, that You will love us and bless us and multiply us and bless the fruit of my/her womb abd that neither male nor female among Your people would be barren."

"Father, we are redeemed from the curse of the Law by Jesus and being barren is under the curse of the Law; therefore, we will receive from Your grace and have children."

"Father, no plague, no evil shall come nigh our dwelling. We are healed by the stripes of Jesus. Sickness of any kind is taken out of our midst. You said to ask anything of You in Jesus' name and it would be done; and that if two of us on earth agree as touching anything it would be done. So we pray and we agree with You and Your Word, Father, that we will conceive and bring forht a healthy, precious baby to Your glory and honour. We pray all this according to Your Word and will. You said, This is the confidence that we have in You, that if we ask anything according to Your will, Your hear us; and if You hear us, we know we have the petition we desire of You. We have it now. Thank You, Father, in Jesus' name."

PRAYER POINTS

1. I claim redemption from curse in childbirth - including pains.
2. I break myself loose from the bondage of fear in childbirth.
3. I speak to each part of my body and command it to live up in God's perfect working order.
4. I command my body to come in line and I agreement with the Word of God.
5. I cast down fear of barrenss in Jesus' name.
6. I declare the curse of barreness broken in Jesus' name.
7. I overide all that doctors have said concerning my conception in the name of Jesus.
8. I command every part of my reproductive system to confrom to the Word of God and plan of God in the name of Jesus.

Prayer made the sun stand still.

9. I cry unto you in the name of the Lord, my body!, conceive in the name of Jesus.
10. I cry unto you in the name of the Lord, my womb!, be pregnant in the name of Jesus.
11. I claim perfect ovulation, release of perfect eggs from the ovaries through fallopin tubes, fertilised by sperms, penetrated healthy pregnancy.
12. I pray for good solid attachment to uterine walls, nourished and protected for 9 months.
13. I claim unharmed and unhindered pregnancy in the name of Jesus.
14. I pray that the pregnancy grows to perfect baby in Jesus' name.
15. Let the pregnancy be fulfilled in the name of Jesus.
16. I decree it in Jesus' name and receive God's best.
17. I would not settle for anything less in the name of Jesus.

 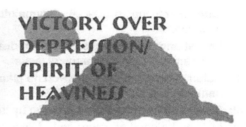

VICTORY OVER DEPRESSION/ SPIRIT OF HEAVINESS

97

Confession: Isa. 61:3, Neh. 8:10, James 4:7, John 14:27, Jer. 29:11, 2 Tim. 1:7, Isaiah 26:3
Song: "Count Your Blessings"

PRAYER POINTS

1. Thank God for His love for you .
2. Thank God for the great and mysterious opportunities of your life.
3. I resist and bind every spirit of oppression and heaviness in the name of Jesus.
4. Let every root of spiritual heaviness and depression in my life dry up in the name of Jesus.
5. Let the Blood of the Lord Jesus Christ close every gate I have opened to any spirit of oppression forever in the name of Jesus.
6. Lord Jesus, walk back into my past and heal all wounded memories and emotions.
7. Let God arise and scatter all that threatens my spiritual welfare in the name of Jesus.
8. Lord, direct and control every movement of my mind.
9. Lord, teach me to use all circumstances of my life today to bring forth the fruit of holiness rather than the fruits of sin.

Prayer is a perpetual force against all powers of darkness.

10. Lord, teach me to use all disappointments as material for patience.
11. I resist and bind every spirit of fear, discouragement, self-pity and depression in the name of Jesus.
12. Satan, I resist you and give you no place or opportunity in the name of Jesus.
13. I claim deliverance from opression by the blood of the Lamb.
14. I Claim the spirit of power and of love and of a calm and well-balanced mind in the name of Jesus.
15. Holy Ghost, incubate my life with your freshness and refreshing power.
16. I cut myself off from any power supplying the rivers of sorrow into my soul in the name of Jesus.
17. I reject every evil command and demon-inspired spiritual prostration in the name of Jesus.
18. I arise from the shell of heaviness and depression in the name of Jesus.
19. I claim total deliverance for my mind in the name of Jesus.
20. Thank you Lord for setting me free from every evil work.
21. Pray in the spirit for sometimes.

Prayer alters people on the inside.

POWER AGAINST EVIL CONSUMPTION

This is a Self-Deliverance Exercise. It should be done Violently and Aggressively.

Confess these scriptures out loud: Psl. 27:1-2, 1 Cor. 10:21, Psalm 91

Praise Worship.

PRAYER POINTS

1. I command every evil plantation in my life, come out with all your roots in the name of Jesus! *(Lay your hands on your stomach and keep repeating the emphasized area.)*

2. Evil strangers in my body, come all the way out of your hidding places in the name of Jesus.

3. I disconnect any conscious or unconscious linkage with demonic cateerers in the name of Jesus.

4. Let all avenues of eating or drinking spiritual poisons be closed in the name of Jesus.

5. I cough out and vomit any food eaten from the table of the devil in the name of Jesus. *(Cough them out and vomit them in faith. Prime the expulsion).*

6. Let all negative materials circulating in my blood stream be evacuated in the name of Jesus.

Prayer unites the souls to God.

7. I drink the blood of Jesus. *(Physically swallow and drink it in faith. Keep doing this for some time.)*

8. Let all evil spiritual feeders warring against me drink their own blood and eat their own flesh.

9. I command all demonic food utensils fashoined against me to be roasted in the name of Jesus.

10. Holy Ghost fire, circulate all over my body.

11. I command all physical poisions inside my system to be neutralized in the name of Jesus.

12. Let all evil assingments fashoined against me through the mouth gate be nullified in the name of Jesus.

13. Let all spiritual problems attached to any hour of the night be cancelled in the name of Jesus. *(Pick the periods from 12 midnight down to 6:00 a.m).*

14. Bread of heaven, fill me till I want no more.

15. Let all cateering equipments of evil cateerers attached to me be destroyed in the name of Jesus.

16. I command my digestive system to reject every evil command in the name of Jesus.

17. Let all satanic designs of oppression against me in dreams and visions be frustrated in the name of Jesus.

18. I remove my name from the register of evil feeders with the blood of Jesus.

19. Let the habitation of evil cateerers become desolate in the name of Jesus.

PRAYER POINTS

1. I pull down the stronghold of confusion in my life in the name of Jesus.
2. Every seat of confusion in my life, be broken down in the name of Jesus.
3. Let the storm of confusion within my mind be still in the name of Jesus.
4. Every cloud of confusion that has enveloped my mind, fade away now in the name of Jesus.
5. I reject every storm of confusion, and claim a sound mind in the name of Jesus.
6. Every power that wants to destroy my life, I command you to be destroyed in Jesus' name.
7. Every faulty foundation in my life, receive the fire of God in the name of Jesus.
8. I fire back every arrow of mind destruction fired into my life back to the sender in the name of Jesus.
9. My mind, receive divine touch of God and be relieved in the name of Jesus.
10. Lord strengthen me in my inner mind with Your fire and Your power in the name of Jesus.

Prayer is acting with God in this battle against evil.

11. I pull down every stronghold of uncontrollable thought in my life in the name of Jesus.
12. I cast down every evil imagination in my heart in the name of Jesus.
13. I bring into captivity every area of my thought life to the obedient of Christ in the name of Jesus.
14. I break the power of evil remote control over my thought in the name of Jesus.
15. I seal off every doorway of evil uncontrollable thought in my life with the blood of Jesus in Jesus' name.
16. I scatter into pieces every evil imagination against me in the name of Jesus.
17. I command all imaginations contrary to my prayer life to be defeated in the name of Jesus.
18. I cast down and bring to nougbt every demonic imagination against me and my family in Jesus' name.
19. I immune my spirit, soul and body against every vain imagination in the name of Jesus.
20. I cast out, plunder and frustrate every satanic imagination against my life in the name of Jesus.
21. Lord, I pull down every stronghold of the enemy over my life in the name of Jesus.
22. I pull down and roast every demonic ladder the enemy is using to climb into my life in the name of Jesus.
23. I come against every evil pronouncement made against my life in the name of Jesus.
24. I arrest and bind every satanic notebook written against my life in the name of Jesus.
25. I cancel and nullify every imagination of enemy upon my life in the name of Jesus.
26. I take captive every evil thought in my heart in the name of Jesus.

Prayer can push out satan from any ground he has gained.

27. Blood of Jesus, cleanse my heart from every evil thought in the name of Jesus.
28. My heart be delivered from every evil thought in the name of Jesus.
29. I shield my heart with the fire of God from every evil thought in the name of Jesus.
30. Heavenly thoughts, fill my heart in the name of Jesus.
31. You my mind, in the name of Jesus, you will not push me to hell.
32. You habitation of darkness in my heart, be desolate in the name of Jesus.
33. Every evil attack on my mind, be defeated in the name of Jesus.
34. You my mind, receive the touch of fire of God in the name of Jesus.
35. In the name of Jesus, I will make it in life.
36. I command satanic table upon which he exhibits its evil in my heart to receive the fire of God in Jesus' name.
37. Sting of death, relaease my mind in the name of Jesus.
38. Sting of fear and failure, release my mind in the name of Jesus.
39. I command every heavy burden in my mind to roll away and be burnt to ashes in the name of Jesus.
40. Blood of Jesus, replenish my heart in the name of Jesus.
41. You powers that corrupt my desire and my mind, be roasted in the name of Jesus.
42. You strongman of evil imagination paralysing the good things in my life, be paralysed in the name of Jesus.
43. Lord, preserve my mind with Your fire in the name of Jesus.
44. Lord, put Your laws into my mind in the name of Jesus.
45. All the good thoughts that the strongman has paralysed in my life, receive life and be restored back into my life in the name of Jesus.

Prayer is a spiritual bombing.

46. I locate every evil tree in my mind with the fire of God in the name of Jesus.
47. I uproot every hidden evil tree in my mind in the name of Jesus.
48. You evil fruit in my life, die in the name of Jesus.
49. You planter of evil tree in my life, be roasted in the name of Jesus.
50. Lord, begin to plant good things in my life and let the good fruits begin to manifest.
51. I bind and cast down the spirit of uncertainty in my mind and I render its activity null and void in my life in the name of Jesus.
52. Holy Ghost, occuppy every area vacated by spirit of uncertainty in my mind in the name of Jesus.
53. Lord, every damage spirit of uncertainty has done in my life be repaired and restored in the name of Jesus.
54. I refuse to give space to spirit of uncertainty in my life in the name of Jesus.
55. I recover and posses every good thing lost to the spirit of uncertainty in the name of Jesus.
56. Throughtout the days of my life, the gate of hell shall not prevail over my life in the name of Jesus.
57. You power of hell, release all my belongings that are under your control in the name of Jesus.
58. As for me and my house, our names will not enter the kingdom of hell in the name of Jesus.
59. You spirit of death, you will not prosper in my life in the name of Jesus.
60. I release the life of Christ into my life in the name of Jesus.
61. My mind, I command you to think alright in the name of Jesus.
62. All mind control spirits, be bound in the name of Jesus.
63. You producer of evil thought in my life, somersault and die in the name of Jesus.

Prayer breaks down every opposing wall.

64. Holy Spirit, renew my mind to glorify God in the name of Jesus.

65. Lord, soak my mind with heavenly revelations.

66. I gathered together every area of my mind that have been scattered in the name of Jesus.

67. Every area of my life and area of my mind in satanic cage, be released in the name of Jesus.

68. I plead the blood of Jesus into my mind and into the whole of my life.

69. I fire back every arrow of the enemy fired into my life in the name of Jesus.

70. I command you my mind, go back to your resting place in the name of Jesus.

CLEANSING AND PURGING OF THE MIND

71. O Lord, help me to locate any spiritual disease in my mind. I release myself from the grip of the spirit of

1. Pride	13. Carnal Imaginations
2. Vanity	14. Deception
3. Greed	15. Wicked Imaginations
4. Fear	16. Ignorance
5. Violence	17. Condemnation
6. Worry	18. Arrogance
7. Envy	19. Forgetfulness
8. Lazyness	20. Mind Blankness
9. Depression	21. Mind Darkness
10. Confusion	22. Mind Dullness
11. Self-importance	23. Turmoil
12. Bitterness	24. Incoherence

72. Father in the name of Jesus, I invite the ministry of deliverance into my mind.

Prayer demolishes every fortress of hell.

73. You powers of darkness, loose your control over my mind in the name of Jesus.
74. Let my carnal mind which is at war with God be conquered and be at peace with God in the name of Jesus.
75. I cast down every vain imagination working against my mind in the name of Jesus.
76. Let every wild, untamed and restless thoughts be captured and brought into submission under the feet of Christ.

Prayer demolishes every fortress of hell.

PRAYERS FOR TRAVELLERS

Confess Psalms 121 and 24

PRAYER POINTS

1. I thank You Lord because the earth is the Lord's and the fulness thereof.
2. Father, bless all my preparations - my passport, visas, my packing - in the name of Jesus.
3. Father, guide me in my choice of company and seating position in the name of Jesus.
4. I paralyse all drinkers of blood and eaters of flesh in the nane of Jesus.
5. I soak myself, my trasport vessel in the blood of Jesus.
6. Let the hedge of fire from the Lord surround me.
7. I shall not die but live to declare the works of God.
8. Let every enemy of the smoothness of my journey be completely paralysed in the name of Jesus.
9. I command darkness to envelope the camp of evil observers and monitoring agents in the name of Jesus.
10. I receive immunity against the perils of roads and dangers from careless people in the name of Jesus.
11. Lord, let me take good care to be responsible.

Overloaded hearts are weak prayer warriors.

12. Lord, help me and give me wisdom to keep my vehicle road worthy.
13. I reject and stand against temptation to drive carelessly in the name of Jesus.
14. Lord, shapen my vision and my sense of judgement.
15. Lord, give me patience and alertness.
16. My transport vessel will not become a coffin in the name of Jesus.
17. Father, let me go without anxiety and come back with satisfaction in the name of Jesus.
18. I claim divine favour at the borders in the name of Jesus.
19. Let my luggages be soaked in the blood of Jesus.
20. O Lord, station Your Holy Angels all around me as I travel (Heb. 1:14).
21. Lord, I pray a wall of fire around myself, fellow-trvellers and the trasport vessel in the name of Jesus.
22. Lord, keep all human "Achans" and "bad feet" away from our transport vessel.

 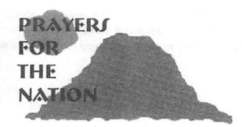

PRAYERS FOR THE NATION

PRAYER POINTS

1. Let righteousness flow like water and truth like an everlasting flowing stream in this country in Jesus' name.
2. Bind and cast out the spirit behind corruption in this country.
3. Wrestle and bind the spiritual strongman in control of Nigeria.
4. Pray for the advancement of the Gospel of our Lord Jesus Christ in this country.
5. Pray against and bind the spirit behind occultic groups, false religions, confraternities, human worship and spiritual politics.
6. Break the yoke of traditional religion.
7. Pray for the crumbling economy and for stable political life.
8. Destroy every stronghold of the power of darkness in the land.
9. Pray against the spirit of the bondwoman and his operation in Nigeria.
10. Come against and resist the spirit of tribalism and sectional sentiments in Nigeria.
11. Destroy the spirit of destruction and molestation of human lives.
12. Let every demonic ethnic, cultural and traditional bondage break.

Prayers are deathless.

13. Arrest and destroy the satanic notion that public offices are meant for personal enrichment.

14. Pray for revival amongst churches in this country.

Made in United States
North Haven, CT
10 May 2024

52374697R00124